MORE THAN MONEY,

A Wholistic Guide…To Having It All

TRUE PROSPERITY

MORE THAN MONEY,

A Wholistic Guide...To Having It All

TRUE PROSPERITY

MICHAEL J. ROADS

books of empowerment

SilverRoads

PUBLISHING

For information write:

SilverRoads Publishing

3029 Prospect Avenue East

Cleveland, OH 44115

Or call: 216.588.0099

Fax: 216.391.1636

email: info@silverroads.com

Web site: http://www.silverroads.com

If you are unable to order this book from your local book-
seller, you may order directly from the publisher.
Quantity discounts for organizations are available.
Call 1.866.409.3434 toll-free.

Library of Congress Catalog Card Number: 2004104627

ISBN 0-9729145-2-8

Copy editing by Carol Schrecengost
Cover design by Susan Miller
Printed by Sheridan Books, Ann Arbor, MI

10 9 8 7 6 5 4 3 2

DEDICATION

When two people have been happily married for over forty-five years, and I place emphasis on 'happily,' then dedicating a book does not need much soul searching. My life today is one of true prosperity, and my wife Treenie is part of that richness. This book is for my beloved Treenie.

CONTENTS

ACKNOWLEDGEMENTS

The first person whom I must acknowledge is Russell, my youngest son. After one of my weekend seminars on True Prosperity, which he attended, he said, "Dad, the next book that you write must be about true prosperity. It must not be one of your story/teaching books. I want you to write it in just the same way that you speak it. If you do this, Dad, it'll be a best seller."

So, here it is, and thank you Russ. This is the first book I have written in this style, and knowing how you have enjoyed it, I'm glad I lived up to your expectations.

As always, I thank my wife, Treenie, for having such utter confidence in my writing ability. When a person believes in you to the extent that she believes in me, it allows you to easily extend yourself into ways of writing that you have never tried before.

To James Silver, my dear friend and partner, from my heart, thank you.

INTRODUCTION

This is not just another book about wealth. Wealth, as such, is incredibly overrated. Wealth, we are led to believe, is the panacea for all problems, the single greatest solution. Right now, in front of me, I have a few of the many wealth seminar adverts: "Enjoy the status of a millionaire." "Make enough money to be secure for life." Really! Money can do all that? I do not think so. True security is based in a strong inner sense of self. False security is based in money. And status? Surely first and foremost, status is about value and worth as a human Being. Life is infinitely deeper than money, and has a far greater meaning. Without a doubt money is the most sought after solution to life's hardships, and fair enough, in some cases it is just what is needed. This book, however, seeks to reveal a deeper meaning to the issues of finance and prosperity. It takes a more wholistic approach to a subject that has as many different facets and complications as there are people involved.

Both my *Chambers Mid-Century* (20th) *Dictionary* and my modern dictionary come up with the same meaning for prosperity: "To get on; to experience favourable circumstances; to flourish and thrive; to turn out well; good fortune; successful; in a very healthy way." Do you notice something? There is no mention of money. Yet money is a human obsession.

One of the more common approaches to money is through the fear of not having enough. Not that many people would admit to this, but for most the fear is there, always lurking in the background. When a high income is achieved, does this dispel the fear of not having enough? Or does it simply overlay it with the deception of security, albeit a temporary one; a situation subject to the whims of workplace instability? Wealth is equated with success in today's tunnel vision society, a blinkered approach fraught with danger. One of our local business men, hailed as wealthy and successful, is struggling to recover from a massive heart attack. That's success? Right now, I think he would readily trade wealth and success for good health and failure. Right now, the prospect of being able to have another go at life, this time including his health as part of his overall prosperity, would surely be very attractive to him.

Even the terms success and failure are fraught with deception. What is success? Is dying unhappy but wealthy, successful? Is living happy and healthy on a low income, failure? There are many questions that are generally overlooked in the drive and strive for wealth. For many people wealth holds hands with social acceptance, with admiration and respect. And for many people these benefits are seemingly necessary. Once enmeshed in the roller coaster of wealth, it becomes increasingly stressful, forever chasing a shadow that is both elusive and beyond your final control. It often seems that other factors conspire against you.

This book takes a far different approach. It takes the meaning of prosperity for what it truly is. If wholeness and happiness have any meaning to you, this is your book. If self-respect, personal health, and your spiritual life have any meaning to you, this is your book. If living a life of harmony, balance, and abundance appeals to you, this is your book. If the quality of life is more important to you than material quantity, this book is for you. This book is not about the money markets, nor is it about financial manipulation. It is about *you*, the person. The asset development in this book looks at *you* as the asset. This book looks at the bigger picture. It acknowledges that, for better or worse, *you* are the creator of your whole life, including your prosperity and abundance.

The intention of this book is to make it better!

True prosperity includes your emotional well-being, your mental balance, and your physical health, as well as a sound financial platform.

1 WHAT IS TRUE PROSPERITY?

A WAY OF LIFE

True prosperity is about you, the person, not the money. Consider a couple of questions: Which occupies your attention the most; the acquisition of wealth, or your everyday integrity? Which is the most important to you; the emotional, mental, and spiritual well-being of you and your family, or simply meeting your and their financial wants and expectations? And I did say 'wants,' not needs. With a focus on the former needs are met, while a focus on the latter simply breeds more wants.

True prosperity is a way of living. It could be aptly described as the art of living. It is broad-based, wholistic, and fully supportive of your life, and living. True prosperity propagates abundance, for life flows most easily along the path of least resistance. To be truly prosperous you are required to learn about some of the Principles of Truth, and you learn how to apply them. These Principles are multilayered. You apply the layer that is most apparent and as this becomes integrated into your life, and as you grow as a human Being, another layer, hitherto unsuspected, reveals itself. There is no real mystery to these Principles, but neither are they shouted from the rooftops. If you live life in a superficial way, you do not encounter them, nor do you if your whole focus is on material wealth. Even the desire to be recognized as successful, or a celebrity, or any consuming ambition, requires so much focus and drive toward the chosen field of your endeavor, you are less available for life's serendipitous encounters with a deeper wisdom. There is, of course, one exception, and that is a focus on attaining such inner wisdom. But this is the choice of the few. The rewards are elusive, and the journey is not so much one of acquiring new knowledge as it is of letting go of all the deep, false, subconscious conditioning. It is, in many ways, a life of surrender, attracting derision rather than accolades from the general public. This was my choice, a way of life, one of many, and we are all free to choose.

THOSE WHO GIVE

The problems with money, both too much or not enough, beset most of the world's population. Without a doubt most people, given a choice, would choose to experience too much money, and yet the paradox is, you do create your own reality, and most people by far have chosen not enough money. I certainly did. And if you had told me about my choosing not enough money in those days, I would have told you what to do with this book! Paradoxes abound. Odd as it may seem, you can more easily learn about true prosperity from the platform of fiscal hardship, than you can from the wealth platform. The wealthy person has a greatly reduced incentive. Not always, but often. They have already translated wealth as success, and success has been their whole focus. To them, they have it made. A powerful illusion. Some of those wealthy people lose touch with the everyday hardships that so many others endure. Statistics from charities indicate that more money is given by those with not enough, than is by those with more than they need. Of course there are many exceptions to this, very many, but the tendency is there. The people who struggle financially have more compassion for people who are without. Understandably so, they live with it.

EARLY INFLUENCES

Whether we like it or not, you and I have a history. We have a childhood behind us that both created and developed the way we approach life. We were all left with the powerful impressions of our parents, and their struggles with life and living. There is little that illustrates this more graphically than their relationship with money. I have no doubt that money is probably one of the greatest catalysts in the average person's life. This is where our initial years set the scene. From our impressions of the past, money either looms large, dominating and clouding our life, or it fits easily and comfortably into its proper place. The way our parents were with money often becomes the way we are with money.

For me, it was very uncomfortable! I well remember my family in England, and how I viewed them as a boy. I perceived them as wealthy and mean. In my childish naivety I put the two together. I linked wealth with meanness, an error that took a lot of undoing. I saw my father as wealthy, but having to work hard for it. As was the custom then, my mother did not work. My father drummed it into me that money was hard to come by, that money did not grow on trees. You know the rhetoric, you have heard it. For years I assumed that this was wise; it was not. Those early impressions are the ones that unknowingly shape our lives. I listened to Great Uncle Joe as he shared his anger about his brother William. Twenty-three years earlier William had died owing Joe twenty pennies, and Joe was still angry! Maybe that would equate with twenty U.S. dollars today, big deal, but Joe's anger was an energy that left a strong negative impression in me.

4

GRASP AND HOLD

Money makes you mean. Over and over this was imprinted into my psyche by a generation of family that knew only how to grasp and hold. Looking back, I realize that most of them lived on inherited wealth. Maybe they inherited the fear that accompanied it, and as I will show you, we do inherit such subtle factors. We inherit not only through family characteristics, but also through impression and repetition; even through reaction and resistance. Of course, the negative influences always have a positive counter-balance, and for me this was embodied by my Great Aunt Polly. She was a wonderful woman, filled with open-hearted generosity and love. She had a sister, my paternal grandmother. I remember one year, I was around eight years of age, my brother around eleven, and our grandmother gave us a clockwork train for Christmas. Very nice, but we were never allowed to have it. We could not take it home, nor could we play with it without grudging permission. Like the Christmas crackers in her house, the toy could be looked at, but not touched. I often wonder who destroyed the child within my grandmother, and how.

NEGATIVE IMPRESSIONS

These stories are in the childhood of every adult. Mine are mild, very mild, compared to some of the shocking stories of deprivation I have listened to. But anything that leaves an impression in your childhood is going to rewrite the same, or a similar story in your adult life. Unfortunately it is the negative stories that you most constantly revisit in your memories; the negatives that you later revitalize into your life. It is the negative impressions that have the most powerful repeat factor, paradoxically the impressions that you least want to retain. Your childhood and growing years are overfilled with the stimuli of life, all stored, filed away, and ready to be withdrawn into shaping the substance of your developing life. Yet all so subtle, so low level, so very subconscious that most people still do not realize that they are the author of their personal lives. You write the full story. You determine your fortune, your drive toward wealth, your attitude toward it, your fears, desires and emotions.

EMOTIONAL ATTACHMENTS

Anything that has had an effect on you in the years of your shaping is going to be emotionally charged. Always! Sad or happy, angry, reactive, or just plain frightened, it is with you all the time. The past is no longer past, for while it affects your adult life you continue to live it. This brings us to the Principles of Truth. One of those

Principles puts it this way: Anything of the past unresolved, is unresolved now. You really do not grow up and leave your childhood behind; you have a body that ages as the years pass by, and a belief that it is the future we need to be concerned with, not the past. Very few people *actively realize* that your future is built on the foundation of your past, and that while negative emotional reactions are still festering within you the toxins continue to pollute your potential. This is not new knowledge, it is well-known and documented, but very few people *consciously engage* such knowledge. With this book, it is my intent that you will build a new and vital structure into your life that is not in any way a repeat, or a reaction, to the negative influence of a person, people, or situations of your childhood.

FAR REACHING

As you may realize, I am only skimming the surface of childhood influences. To plumb at depth would require a book in its own right. Your time spent with your parents, your siblings, particularly your years at school, all are going to affect the quality of your life now. In my case, my years at school had a huge affect on me emotionally, and today I can clearly see how it influenced me, both positively and negatively. For now, I simply wish to draw attention to this period of intense subconscious pro-gramming, so you are aware that true prosperity is not simply about the acquisition of money. I want you to see that true prosperity is far reaching in its implications. True prosperity includes your emotional well-being, your mental balance, and your physical health, as well as a sound financial platform. On this basis you can plant your feet firmly and confidently, creating anew not only for yourself, but also creating newness for all those people within your sphere of influence. This happens, whether you invite it or not.

Sphere of influence

Just as you were affected by the influence of your parents, grandparents, and other relatives, so you in turn become a sphere of influence for other people. First in line are your own children. It would be good to ensure that the influences that penetrate them are beneficial, uplifting, creating a positive foundation on which they will build their lives. One way or the other, you *will* affect them. You have no choice about this. Your choice is about the quality of that influence. You and your spouse/partner decide whether your children are imprinted with impressions of value, or whether their youthful anger and reaction to you compels them to take aboard your own inherited 'junk.' And in turn, to pass it on.

One of the aspects of true prosperity is to break these negative cycles, while creating and/or reaffirming positive ones. What an inheritance this is. Seriously, this has far greater value than purely money-based inherited wealth. Anyone can give their children a legacy of immense richness, without any money at all. Be aware of what you strive for in life. Ask yourself where you find the *real* things of life, and how much the purchase price was. If the purchase price is your caring, focussed attention to your children and whole family, then everybody in the family benefits. Truly, you have purchased very wisely!

NATURAL RESPONSIBILITY

In the final analysis, you and I are each responsible for our lives. Your children will be responsible for theirs. You can make their task easier, or far more difficult. To me, that is the natural responsibility of being a parent. The negative influences I picked up were not given to me deliberately, and if my grandmother and great uncles could read these words I am sure they would be shocked. I have prospered from the influence of my Great Aunt Polly. This was her legacy to me, but I did not receive this from my grandmother. An acquaintance of mine inherited wealth from his father, along with a greedy negative attitude. It illustrates the difference between inherited prosperity not involving money, and inherited money not involving beneficial attributes. Inherited wealth along with inherited bad attitudes is a seriously miserable inheritance. I am sure that most people give little thought to the non-fiscal legacies, yet if life's values have any real meaning for you, these values will be of great benefit as your focus and purpose in life.

MORE THAN WORDS

Let me clarify this just a little further. The words you share with your family, the conversations you have, all have an effect on shaping your children's future. Especially the words spoken carelessly, or in anger, or in reaction. But by far the greatest impact comes from your actions. Do your actions support your words, or do you speak one set of values for your children, while you are living a far more negative reality? The standard you *live* becomes the foundation on which they build. So often a teenager screams with anger at a parent, accusing them of hypocrisy. And they are right. Parental hypocrisy is very common, but it is not a crime, seldom intentional, nor am I pointing a finger. All I want to emphasise is that it becomes part of your children's inheritance. For them, your actions become either a positive brick in a foundation of true prosperity, or a negative brick in the wall they build around themselves. None of this is right or wrong, not even good or bad, it is simply about the way lives are built, maintained, expanded, or shattered. And right now far too many young lives are getting shattered.

LOTTERIES: HOPELESS HOPE

This background of your so-called past is the murmur in your everyday life. By far the greatest reaction to unhappiness is to strive for wealth. I find this to be amazing, but very understandable. Today, we are being conditioned that wealth equates with happiness. Lotteries in particular promote this concept daily through the media, with emphasis on television. You get to see the happy faces of the winners! And people believe this stuff. The temptation of huge wealth is chased by people burdened with the illusion that this will make them happier. Kennon Sheldon, a psychologist at the University of Missouri in Columbia, states: "We consistently find that the people who say that money is most important to them are the unhappiest." Americans spend more than $25 billion a year on lottery tickets. That is a high price for hopeless hope. It means just a few financial winners, with a huge number of losers. That's the gamble.

Consider the odds. The 6/51 U.S. lottery is 18 million to 1 against you. Some odds! Truly, there are better ways to approach financial problems than through the 'quick fix' dream. One study found that instant millionaires are no happier than recent accident victims. They suffer massive disillusionment. The money is not the problem, it is the human factor. This is why I am crafting a book that offers far more intelligence than wealth equals success equals happiness. That is about as misguided as one can get, plus it carries a nasty sting in its tail. When the bewildered victim lashes out, it poisons other people in the immediate vicinity. And it gets passed on! It holds repercussions of disillusionment, of discord, and of shattered expectations.

THE PERSON, NOT THE MONEY

If the winner sees their security in money, they have lessons piling up further along the road of life. If they see this as a blessing that, wisely used, can enhance the quality of their life, they become a true winner. And everyone thinks that this is them! Those who understand that money is no more than a tool of wealth hold a great potential to experience true prosperity. Those who believe that the money itself is prosperity have a minefield of disappointments to negotiate. Money will not solve your problems. While you retain the habits that created your problems it will not even solve your financial ones. At best it will be a temporary band aid.

BOTH WITH AND WITHOUT

I give five-day retreats and seminars in many countries of the world. I meet a lot of very wealthy people. My overall impression is that for the majority the only problem that they do not have is money. As I said, they have wealth, but very, very few have true prosperity. Mostly, they have relationship and emotional problems, particularly with their spouses and/or children. Now, I am not suggesting that this is exclusive to them, we know better, but many of these people rest on their laurels, unwilling to contemplate the huge cost in human terms that they have paid for their so-called success. I repeat, true prosperity embraces the wholeness and fullness of life; it is not a wealth-based achievement.

Having said this, I need to add that I meet a lot of people who are continually living on the edge of financial hardship. They also have emotional and relationship problems. Generally, the more aware of these people are more likely to seek help. Generally, they are less able to afford professional help, but are more likely to seek it. Generally, they read books less inclined toward becoming an instant millionaire, more inclined toward broad-based self-improvement. I emphasise *generally* because I do not like the all-inclusive sweeping statement. We are too much of a mixed bag to be over categorized. All I am attempting here is to place before you some of my observations about people and money. We come in many facets. Sadly, I have no doubt that the largest majority of people with financial hardship do nothing but grumble and blame, pointing a finger at other people and the current government. The person locked in blaming is the classic victim. They are difficult to reach, until they realize that *they personally* are their own problem.

Deeper issues

In this book I can only address issues for the people who reach out. It is ironic that the very wealthy think they have no need, while people in poverty become ensnared in their own suffering. How ironic it is that apathy immobilizes both ends of the human spectrum of wealth and poverty. Strange, that apathy should be a shared companion, yet seldom do the people on either end have a glimpse of this.

A friend was telling me recently about some of the retired British wealthy living the 'good' life in the South of Spain. They have all that they need, along with an abundance of 'toys' and things they do not need. And in this luxury . . . they wait to die. He told me that so many of them were utterly bored. Some freely confessed it. "Just waiting to die, old son."

Bridge parties, tennis, swimming, rounds of cocktail parties, on and on, waiting, while trying not to wait! "They have plenty of wealth," he told me, "but in conversation with some of them I realized that they have lived their life devoid of inner fulfillment. Most either don't realize it, or don't want to. Some admit it, with regret, sighing about how it's too late now."

Inner fulfillment is a treasure for which to give blessings. It holds the substance and meaning of true prosperity. A person who retires from work fulfilled, knowing that this fulfillment was not work-based, nor money-based, nor even achievement-based, is a person you should meet and talk with. This is a person who has much to offer. To spend time with a person who has based their inner fulfillment in their own value as a human Being, nourishing and nurturing their inner self, would be time exceptionally well spent. Such a person would beneficially touch the lives of everyone in their family and circle of friends. And the beautiful thing is, there are many such people.

SKILLS TO BE LEARNED

True prosperity is about the abundance of life. A child knows what this abundance is. A child does not look at the world through a framework of money, they look through the eyes of wonder. Life is a mystery to them, it is exciting, a daily gift waiting to be lived. At least, that is what is natural to them, that is their potential. Overindulged children quickly lose it. They turn from the wonder of everyday life, to having their daily expectations met. They move from the immense creativity gained by amusing themselves, to needing to be continually entertained. With unaware parents, wealth quickly erodes the meaning of the child's life, and they grow up with a program of expectations that will eventually destroy the quality of their life. Equally, parents who are financially burdened will often sacrifice all to give their children the latest designer clothes and designer toys they crave. Such a sacrifice seldom engenders lifelong appreciation, nor does it create worthwhile values.

Giving to yourself, and to your family, in a way that has lasting benefits is a skill that needs to be learned. We continually undervalue ourselves as human Beings, while overvaluing the trendy, passing phases of modern society. So much of what we think we need is of no value at all, while the development of inner qualities is all too easily ignored. This is not the way of true prosperity. You are important, you and your family as people. You are unique. It is that uniqueness that needs to be nurtured and developed.

SUMMARY

You have a far greater potential than you realize. You *can* live within a framework of true prosperity. With wisdom, you can do this in a wholistic way, developing the skills required. This is not about effort, it is about attention. It is not about being clever, it is about being focussed. It is not about grumbling over what you cannot do, it is about developing what you can. True prosperity is about you. You were born to be abundant - truly - the main skill you have to learn is to cease the denial of this.

*W*hen you focus on your higher, finer qualities, you attract opportunities for these to develop and grow.

2 *LIVING IN A DIFFERENT WAY*

ADAPTABILITY

It is said that humans are among the most adaptable of all creatures. I am not sure that I agree with this. I have no doubt about our ability to adapt, but the actual changes required are so very often resisted. Rats, now they really can adapt, and without a whole lot of intellectual and emotional resistance! But us, we are so very habitual, and habits strongly resist change. As crazy as it may seem, poverty can - and does - become a habit. Being out of work can become a habit. Living on the welfare cheque can become so habitual that it can pass from one generation to another, until five generations of a family have lived in this way. While the original welfare recipient adapted their lifestyle to handle impoverishment, it became an established way of life, part of their legacy to their following generations. Adaptability is about constant change and flux, continually adapting to new circumstances.

Adaptability is about inner flexibility. It is about inner

movement; the ability to flow with the circumstances of life with the least possible resistance. This is quite an asset. If you are an adaptable person then you can certainly achieve true prosperity and abundance. If you are currently fixed and stuck in a situation, but open enough to reach out to a book like this, then you have the adaptability to break the stranglehold you are in.

THE FIRST STEP

You have to take the first step toward helping yourself. You have to let go of old, outmoded patterns of behaviour that are clearly not working for you, and move on. If the way that you are living holds you away from true prosperity, then you need to know a better way, a more uplifting way. I have talked to many people during my True Prosperity seminars, and I have heard a huge range of reasons why people live with hardship. Most begin with their parents, with their upbringing, and with their inherited belief systems. Even the belief systems expressed by the media have a huge impact. I listened recently to a woman on the radio addressing the issue of local poverty. She apportioned the major share of blame to the state and federal governments for not creating enough jobs. I can see her viewpoint, and what she said has merit, but it points the finger and it maintains blame.

While you see the answers to your financial problems - or any problems - as outside of yourself, then you will never achieve true prosperity. You are responsible for your situation, and until you can accept this there will be no inner movement. Responsibility means the ability to respond. If you have done it inappropriately, it does not make you foolish or bad! It is simply mismanagement.

REACTION OR RESPONSE?

If you react to life's challenges, then you repeat old patterns of fear. The same patterns that your parents had. Fear reacts. To react means a re-enactment of the past. It means you are holding the door closed to new expressions. It means a repeat of anger, blame, and other expressions of fear. Response is quite different. You respond from the moment, not the past. Openness responds. Love responds. Courage responds. All are human attributes that every one of us possess in the moment. You have to learn to be responsive to life, rather than living from your reactions. Response is a positive, forward step; reaction is a negative, backward step. You choose! But, do you? Reaction is not a choice, it is the abdication of choice. To respond is a choice that, literally, continually needs to be chosen. Response can never be automatic, because it is about living from the moment, consciously aware. Reaction is powerfully automatic, all over in a moment, yet often leaving a feeling of deep regret, or guilt.

CARRYING BAGGAGE

Basically, if the way you are now living is not working for you, you need to learn to live in a different way. You need to let go of the baggage that you are carrying, and usually that means identifying it first. Now, this is not about criticism or judgment of yourself. It is about looking clearly at yourself and identifying your strong points and your weak points. I repeat, this does not mean criticising your weak points, it means accepting them, accepting that this is not permanent, and moving on to your strong points. You build true prosperity on your strengths, on acknowledging them, and on creating a structure for the new self on those strengths. By doing this you change and grow. You would be amazed at how many of the once weak points become strengths simply by exposing them to the process of inner change.

Obviously in this process many fears will arise and resistance will be encountered. Some of this will be looked at in this book, but a book cannot do it for you. I am emphasising this for a reason. Several times I have heard a person remark on a book they have read which is designed to help people improve their life skills. "Didn't do much for me though," they have said in a dismissive way. I have challenged this. The person squirms when I point out that the book cannot possibly do anything for them. It can inspire them, ignite them and inform them, but then it has to be applied to their life. "Didn't do much . . ." is the voice of apathy.

A COMMON FACTOR

Probably the greatest single factor which undermines any individual is self-criticism. The root meaning of criticism is 'to consider, or evaluate.' In a modern dictionary however, it has come to mean; 'the act of making an unfavourable judgment.' Most of us grew up with criticism, and unfortunately most of us will pass it on. Criticism is a focus. First, let me be clear about focus. Another of those Principles states: What we focus on is what we attract. So if your focus is self-criticism, then you attract more of the negative aspects which you are already criticising. Meaning, criticism becomes a magnifying lens through which life flows, continually becoming your reality. You create the substance of your life. You can do this negatively or positively. When you do it negatively, wealthy or poor, life becomes a struggle. When you do it positively, the results are far more accommodating for your happiness and well-being. I have yet to meet anyone who enjoys self-criticism, but most people are engaged in this practice for much of the day. Generally it is subconscious chatter, a continual stream of negative self-talk that is an unrealized subliminal program. And nobody wants it. I did it, and I found it difficult to stop. Difficult perhaps, but never impossible. If I could stop it, so can you. The first step is to realize that this is happening. And then not to criticise yourself because it is happening!

POOR COMPANY

Self-criticism and hardship hold hands. Imagine spending a day with a 'friend' who criticises you all day. You meet, and your friend says, "Gee, you look rough. What's happened to you?" From there on it gets worse. Over a cup of coffee your friend tells you what is wrong with you, focussing on your every negative aspect, constantly bringing it to your attention. You go into a clothing shop, and the monologue continues. "Well, you're too fat, aren't you, you didn't really expect that it would fit." Or if you are slim, "Just look at you. It hangs on you like a bag. You need to shape up." And so on, all morning until lunch. "Going to eat fat food, are you? A minute in your mouth and a year on your hips. You know how it is and you know how easily you put weight on." During the afternoon you go to see a movie, so you get a little rest. As you come out your companion starts again. "Well, that was a waste of time! Told you it would be no good. Did you notice Mel is looking older these days. But there, we all age, don't we? Do you notice how jowly you're looking? It's like your jaw's sagging into your neck. Are you feeling all right? You're not ill, are you?"

SELF-DENIAL

That will do. You get the idea. How likely is it that at the end of your day out you would invite this friend home to continue more of the same all evening? You would not! You would willingly punish the 'friend,' but could you even imagine rewarding them? They just ruined your day. But what happens when that 'friend' is your inner critic? What happens when it is *you* who are consciously and subconsciously criticising yourself all day? Sadly, you punish yourself, that is what happens. You do it without any awareness of it happening, but you do it just the same. It is surely no surprise if I tell you that one form of punishment is the denial of prosperity. Wealthy or poor, the punishment will be delivered in the most meaningful way for you. Self-criticism will, and does, maintain financial hardship. And if you are a self-criticising person who wins big on the lottery, the punishment will continue in other ways. It will move from a financial focus into emotional and relationship problems.

Cease the self-criticism. Let go of criticising other people. Stop criticising politicians, governments, presidents, multinationals, the kids . . . the whole long list! Just stop criticising.

FIELD OF ENERGY

Just imagine that you are a field of energy. Of course, you are, but sit quietly, close your eyes and visualize your energy as a huge field of light. Focus into this light a few times and you will realize that there is no true boundary to it. Your physical body has very clear and defined boundaries; like an envelope it ends at the skin, and all the working parts are contained in their own sheaths. But as an energy Being you have a very different reality. We all - each one of us - occupy the same space. Science knows this, and it is very real, but we live and act as though we are all separate. This is one of the mass illusions of humanity. We seem to have an intellectual grasp of the 'web of life' as a concept, but we seem unable to comprehend that this is the everyday reality of our lives. In other words, what I think about you will affect *my* life. Not yours, mine. What you think of the U.S. president, or any world leader, will have a minor effect on them and a major effect on you. If you criticise public figures, you are, in effect, criticising yourself. When you criticise members of your family, you criticise yourself. And you experience the effect! Then, in complete ignorance, you blame it on life, other people, or circumstances. You call yourself unlucky! To experience true prosperity you have to accept that this web of life is reality, and that you are living within it.

A NEW FOCUS

You need to accept that you need new influences in your daily life, new input, a fresh new open approach to life. More of the same is not working well for you. More of the same is the ongoing problem, so a change of focus is needed. A different way of living. One of the assets you need to cultivate is self-respect. Obviously there is no self-respect to be found in self-criticism, just more of the same, driven with as much power and energy as you put into criticising yourself and other people. But that self-talk can be turned right around, facing the direction of self-appreciation. You can develop a focus of seeing everything in yourself, and in other people, that you can verbally appreciate. You need to speak the words, so you, and other people can hear them. With a focus on appreciation, you attract more and more qualities and situations into your, and your family's life, to appreciate. It is so simple. But you have to do it, *live it*, for it to work. Reading these words will not make it happen. It is up to you. If you put more light into the light of self, life gets brighter; the reverse is also true. The heavy shadows of criticism, or the light of appreciation? You chose by *living* your choice.

MORE SHADOW PLAY

Judgment is in the same category as criticism. Most of us who had any religious connections have been raised from childhood with the concepts and words of divine judgment, even divine retribution. Heavy stuff! Now, while I have my own deeper experiences of divinity, it is not the purpose of this book to address such issues. However, I have met so many people with God's judgment as an issue, I am aware of the incredibly nullifying effect this has on many people's lives. They fear God's judgment. They have been brought up by parents who used the term 'God's judgment' as a vehicle through which to pour their own criticism and judgment on other people and the state of the country. A child who hears the government being 'judged' and found guilty, knows nothing of the government or the issues, but they are living within the negative energy field of the parent, and they pick up and *personalize* the judgment and criticism. In their reality it becomes them - the child - who is to blame for some mysterious, but horrendous wrong.

NASTY REPERCUSSIONS

Can we even imagine the long-term negative effects? When the child's whole youth is spent in such energy, a constant ongoing battering of the child's psyche, the scene is set for a lifetime of either dysfunctional wealth, or most often, a life of dysfunctional hardship. Even worse, these people become heavily judgmental of themselves and other people. As I said earlier, everything that most disturbs you as a child gets built into your psyche and repeated. Then, of course, all this holds hands with self-hate. Sadly, this, in turn, leads to serious depression. Depression is the birthplace of most illness. Depression is, or very soon will be, the major sickness of this new century. It is the fundamental cause behind suicides. That is well enough known and documented, the problem lies in getting to the root cause behind the depression. I am not a psychologist. I am an educator. I teach an advanced Art of Living. Advanced enough to peel aside the superficial layers of everyday deceit, and to expose our true and basic humanity; our deeper, quintessential self.

TIME TO RECONSIDER

Life is not about correcting wrongs; that is a negative focus, creating and attracting more so-called wrongs to deal with. Life is about correct focus. When you focus on your higher, finer qualities, you attract opportunities for these to develop and grow. Judgment has no place in this. Not for one moment do I accept that the Divine Essence we label God is in any way judgmental. Religions judge, not God. And religions are people. Take away the people and you have no religion, but you still have God! It boils down to one unavoidable reality; people judge, and judgment is mostly negative.

Let me share one of my observations: If you judge yourself, you will *always* find yourself as guilty, not good enough, wrong. Why? Because innocence *never* judges. Do you see what I am saying? It is impossible for the inner state of innocence to look within and judge self. So an inner state of judgment is already based in self-deceit and falsity; it already holds preconceived guilt. Let go of judging yourself, other people, or life.

INNOCENCE

This brings up another question. What is innocence? Amazingly, there are several languages that do not even have a word for innocent! The nearest they can get is 'not

guilty.' 'Not guilty' and innocent are worlds apart. I suggest that when this book is translated into those languages that the English word 'innocent' is used, regardless of
language. The reader will find its meaning. Innocence is
not based in goodness, or in good acts; innocence is the
complete lack of guile. It is the pure child state within,
uncorrupted by any trace of wants or desires. When you
look at 'innocent' in those terms you begin to realize why
the judicial system uses 'guilty' or 'not guilty' in court.
We all have pure innocence within us, but as a quality
of expression we leave it behind when we grow from our
babyhood. It is that childhood innocence that emerges
when a person is truly in touch with their spiritual essence and rejoices in living it.

NON-ATTACHED

As an adult probably the closest you can get to that
childlike innocence is to be non-attached. To take what
life offers with goodwill, while not needing to chase
material wealth, nor to be overwhelmed by ambition.
This is not to say that you have no need to earn money.
There is a huge difference between meeting your need
and feeding your greed. True prosperity includes
meeting your needs on all your many levels of being,
living in a balanced and positive way. Judgment and

criticism are negatives, both lead to depression. If you judge the world and find it wanting, it is you who will feel depressed, not the world. If you constantly criticise the current governments, it is your quality of life that is negated, not the governments'. Politicians destroy the quality of government simply by the ever-ongoing scale of criticism each political party has for the other parties. Constructive criticism is seldom used. For a politician in opposition to say, "The government is doing a good job, but they could do much better," holds the positive seeds of a creative potential for the politician concerned. Continually saying, "The government is bloody hopeless," becomes the negative input into the politician's life. And it gets to be lived! Of course, they would not agree with this, you may not, but the interconnectedness of all life cares little for what you believe or agree with. The aforementioned Principle clearly states; what you focus on is what you attract and create in your life. Your most constant thoughts and words are your focus. And when you consider the negative anger and blame in so much of society's thinking, it is scary.

BLAME AND PUNISHMENT

So often you see a newspaper headline, "Who's to blame?" Politics, sport, accidents, we always look to apportion blame. Blame and punishment are not an intelligent way to run our society; the focus attracts more of the same. Equally, in your personal life, blame and punishment are negative, punishing focusses. If it was not happening in personal lives, it could not be the expression of the newspapers. It is a sad fact, but the newspapers reflect the people. Unfortunately, blame is a global reality in most people's lives on a daily basis, yet remains completely unrecognized. We are all too contented to live in the illusions of life, seldom prepared to face a greater reality: a reality of responsibility, a reality that accepts that you are responsible for your life. It becomes glaringly obvious that blame and punishment mixed with criticism and judgment are going to create a negative and difficult life, no matter what your financial status is. I would like you to avoid this.

REPETITION

You need to be very clear about this. The scale of blame and punishment, of criticism and judgment, is all about constant repetition. If you give the occasional critical opinion, it matters nothing, it has no power. If you make an occasional judgment while under stress, again, it matters little. Any occasional negative remark or expression has little to no power. It is the constant repetition that negatively empowers it. If you walk into an art gallery and, after a short while walk out declaring it boring, it simply expresses either your lack of art appreciation, or your dislike of that particular exhibition. It matters not at all. If, however, you live in that manner, regularly and strongly opinionated with a negative outlook on people and life in general, then your life will most certainly reflect your negative opinions. For as long as you sustain the thought and/or voiced negative opinions, you attract the substance of that focus into your life. It is as easy to do this with wealth as it is in fiscal hardship.

Constant negative repetition creates and maintains negative habits. Habit becomes your conditioning. This is not a good place to be. Conditioning means that all your energy is subconsciously being focussed to maintain the mess you are making of your life. It means that subconsciously, you are creating self-defeat, and you are never aware of it. Only when it comes into your awareness do you have the chance to break the conditioning.

SUMMARY

It becomes very clear that you are a Being of energy. You attract into your field of energy - your life - all that holds your constant, repetitive focus. A negative focus attracts and maintains a negative life. Happily, the opposite is also true, but if this was the common way I would not be writing this book. Life always responds to needs, and potentially, this book will meet your needs. You need to find a different way to express yourself. You need to dig deeper into your humanness, finding the qualities that have always awaited your caring investigation. You need to learn that a positive appraisal of life attracts and expresses in a way that is both uplifting and energising. And remember, you are required to *live* what you learn. If you do not live it, you have not learned it! You have a choice: shall I live as my own best friend, or shall I be my own worst enemy? You decide.

After all, it is you who decides if it will be a happy movie or sad, filled with love, or drama, or just plain difficult.

3 ABOUT YOUR LIFE-MOVIE

THE JOKE IS ON US

How strange it is that to be positive you have to constantly and consciously choose, while negativity is automatic. But this is your unwitting creation. You were designed with the opposite potential. By design, you are easily uplifted, seeing sunshine instead of clouds, the positive not the negative, moving with rather than against, living by Grace rather than struggle, but you have seriously subverted that design. Odd as it may seem, some people seem to get a perverse pleasure from a negative focus. When I visit the U.K. I often see a friend and his partner. A few years ago my friend collected my wife and I from the airport, and drove us to their home. On the way he talked without break about the negative state of the country. When we got to his home, he continued in this theme for half a day, stating many of the crazy bureaucratic decisions and actions in such a way that he had us shrieking with laughter. Eventually I said to him, "Okay, you have had most of the day telling us the negative things about life in Britain, now tell us some of the positive things." For the next minute or so there was silence. "Well?" I said, expectantly. "I can't think of anything," he finally replied.

It is the brain which finds negative-based humour as funny, prompting our laughter. Movies such as *Home Alone* use this, for all the humour is based in the way the house invaders are repetitively defeated and hurt, their own intent turned against them. I am not saying that this is bad. The movie made me laugh. I am saying that it is head/brain humour, and that the basis of this humour is threat, pain, defeat and humiliation. Not positively creative, is it? The heart laughs when the humour is based in 'We all feel good.'

WHERE TO BEGIN?

Better by far to imprint at a young age on 'feel good' movies rather than 'nasty funny.' Those imprints become part of another movie; the movie of your life. True prosperity is something you programmed into, or out of your life at a very early age. Please be aware of this: for better or worse, what you do about your finances as an adult has already been predetermined by you, all completely unrealized. The good news is that it can be changed. This is precisely what this book is about. It is changed by a far deeper appreciation of yourself as a wholistic Being; meaning, the fullness of your life experience, rather than the issues of the moment. The dichotomy is, your whole life from birth to this moment is the issue of the moment! You are a program for life, programmed by self! And changing the program begins only when you can accept this as reality, not purely conceptual. You may well be thinking, how can I change the past? What do I do? First, look through your childhood and see the triggers for yourself. Learn to identify the program that you have inadvertently created. No criticism, no judgment, just look and see.

MOVIE TIME

I mentioned the movie of your life. Consider a movie such as *War and Peace*. It is a long movie, made up from many thousands of single frames. If I took out one of those frames and asked you to have a good look at it, then tell me what the movie was about, you would protest. One frame would hardly even give a hint at the contents of the movie, and even if it did it would be out of context. Okay, let us look at the movie of your life in exactly the same way. The whole movie is called 'The Continuity of Self.' In this movie, each frame is a single life, and there are many, many frames to the whole movie. Obviously, this leads into very deep speculation, opening up vast areas for metaphysical exploration, but that is not for this book. I need your focus on the movie. This is the movie of *you*. And *you* are the movie producer. *You* put up all the energy required for the movie. *You* are the director. *You* direct the whole movie, every frame. *You* are the scriptwriter. *You* craft the whole story, and *you* plot all that happens. *You* are the casting director. *You* decide who, among the people of the world, will be the actors and players in *your* movie. Both goodies and baddies! Finally, *you* are the 'star.' Yes, *you* are a movie star!

MAKE IT HAPPY

If you can accept yourself as part of an ongoing life-movie, you have taken a big step toward achieving true prosperity. If you think the many, many frames of the life-movie to be fanciful and foolish, then it is going to be that much more difficult for you to make the 'real' changes that are required. I recommend that you use the life-movie as a metaphor through which to approach your life, keeping it in mind for your every situation. Acting from this premise, you will be pleasantly surprised at the differences that begin to appear in your life, especially if you direct the movie in a way that creates greater fulfillment in your life. After all, it is you who decides if it will be a happy movie or sad, filled with love, or drama, or just plain difficult. Personally, I like my movie to be 'happy ever after,' and that is the way it is running. But I do confess to having had an earlier run of drama and trauma.

No time out

Remember, this movie is always running. Even the coffee break is part of the movie! Even when you sleep, consciousness remains active and creative. Bearing this in mind, let us look at a single small, but familiar section of the movie, a part that gets repeated many times. Call it a bit of overwriting! You are in a shop with a friend, browsing the articles for sale. You see something that you have wanted for a long time, so you look at the price. As always, it is expensive. You shrug, sigh, saying to your friend how nice it is, how you have always wanted one. "Buy it," they urge. "Go on, get it." You run the figures hopefully through your mind once more, then sigh again. "I can't afford it," you say, as you turn away. How many times have those words been spoken into your movie? The repetitive factor kicks in. As the scriptwriter of your movie, 'I can't afford' is becoming indelibly imprinted, so much so that *it will continue from one frame of the movie to the next*. Not nice! Every time you talk about that incident, 'I can't afford' will be repeated, over and over. Each time you think about it, the same words repeated. Multiply this by all the items that 'I can't afford' and it is very high on the repetitive negative list.

TOGETHERNESS

'I can't afford' has now become a focus. You attract to yourself more of what you focus on, and this focus is *lack*. The opposite of gain. The very last thing that you want to continue in your life. Nothing that you do physically is going to change that. Not a salary increase, not working day and night, not an inheritance, not a lottery win. Lack will win the day, because you and lack are holding hands. You have created this lack, you are joined with it, married to it, united, and sudden wealth cannot alter that. Sure, it would have a short-term effect in this frame of the movie, but all that you repetitively create continues along with the essential self. You have written 'lack' into your life-movie, and lack has many ways of expressing. This is togetherness in the worst possible way! That is the bad news, but the sun still shines. The good news is, you can easily change it. Just as you have used repetition against you, so you can use it for you.

MORE SHOPPING

Okay, back to the shops with your friend. But this is a new you, practising a new way of focussing. This time you are *not* looking at items that are 'way beyond' your budget. You are no longer reinforcing lack. You are looking at items that may well be a fiscal stretch, but they are in the realm of possibility. And as you browse the shelves, you see something that you want, and can just possibly afford. You take it to the counter, and as you pay for it, no matter whether it is credit card, cheque, or cash, during the money transaction you say aloud to the teller, or your friend, "There's plenty more money where this comes from."

Instead of words of negative financial lack being repeated into your life-movie, there are now continuous words of positive financial gain. Every time you spend any money at all, however much or little, you say aloud, "Plenty more money where this comes from."

I teach this in my True Prosperity seminars, and it makes me smile at how many people get excited as they e-mail me, or personally tell me how well it works. "I just don't understand it," they say. I always explain how and why in the seminars, but the metaphysics of it escapes most people.

FEELS MUCH BETTER

Have you noticed how you feel when you say, "I can't afford"? Your energy slumps, you are negated by your own words. That energy field of Light I have mentioned is dimmed. In fact, your whole energy field slumps, losing its dynamic. You feel the dimming of the Light, and you reluctantly accept your feelings of inadequacy that now arise. This is an old, well-established feeling. One of loss, of being incapable, a feeling so constant that it has become a subconscious murmur of discord somewhere in your background. You have learned to 'tune it out' so you are no longer aware of it on a conscious level, but subconsciously the imprint goes deeper and deeper. It is negative and demeaning, contributing very strongly toward sickness.

Now try a few different words; "Plenty more money where this comes from." Energy lifts, and you feel more positive, more 'I'm okay!' That energy field of Light gets brighter, and you are braced, uplifted, your natural dynamic reinforced. You feel the brightening of the Light, and you have an inner glow as the new program of being adequate and capable is being established. You no longer tune it out, rather you focus on the feelings of well-being that surge through your body and psyche, and you know that this is all going into the continuing movie of your life. It is positive and honouring, contributing toward good health and vitality.

Positive friends

As I have shown, the negative "I can't afford" has been used so often it is now on automatic, so you will have to be constantly focussed and aware when you are shopping. Hold an image of yourself as having a good experience as you walk among the shops, an experience that is uplifting and ongoing. If you are with a friend, choose a friend who is positive in his or her way of being. Choose a friend who enjoys this new outlook on life that you are developing. One who encourages you to say, "Plenty more money where this comes from," and who also wants to practice it. You need supportive and positive friends around you as you move into a new way of life, because habit will oppose you. And never underestimate the harmful power of negative habits, or negative people.

Wrong focus

I have often been asked, why are habits so powerful? Why is negative so easy? It seems strange that a humanity which is naturally positive should spend so much of life in a negative focus. Unfortunately, society functions in a way that is less supportive of the positive than the negative. Governments spend their time and your money arguing about the negatives, thus negative becomes a governmental focus. The media focusses around the negatives, reporting all that is wrong with the world, deepening people's feelings of fear and insecurity. More negative focus. Insecure people talk among themselves, discussing the negative issues of other people, and world situations. We reinforce and support the negatives of life constantly and habitually. How then could you expect a positive focus to be quickly and easily established, when you have become saturated in the negatives of life.

A LITTLE LIFT

Your emotions have far more impact on your life than is generally realized. When your thoughts are constantly negative they create a feeling of depression. Depressed emotions then reinforce the negatives, while the 'feeling' of depression creates a powerful focus for more of the same. All in all, a nasty self-defeating trap. The reality is - you set the trap, and you have to release yourself. Knowing the nature of the trap is where it begins, knowing that mentally and emotionally you need to lift yourself into a higher, lighter space. You need to smile a lot, thinking thoughts that cause you to smile. You can smile at people - they need it - lifting them as you lift yourself. A little lift makes life a whole lot lighter.

This in turn, lifts your emotions, creating an emotional

and mental focus which will make your day lighter and brighter. But, as I have said, you have to 'do' this, and it will require a real effort. You have to begin your day with a decision that this is a new day, and that you are a new person, light and cheerful, and that this will be your focus all day. Do not allow yourself to slip into automatic and negative, you deserve better, but only *you* can deliver better.

AVOID THE TRAP

One of the traps that many people who are new to their spiritual life initially fall into is the conflict between business and spiritual. Let me be clear about this, there is no conflict unless you create it. There are no hard and fast rules to abide by, but you need to know your own inner nature. One man I know who is on his spiritual path has quit being a lawyer because he can no longer work in an industry based around other people's conflict and misery. Yet I know another man on his path who has recently become a lawyer so that he can bring some positive light into work that is based in negatives. Two different men, both opening up to a greater Truth in life, yet each expressing it in very different ways. And both are right for themselves. The idea that you cannot have money and be truly spiritual is nonsense, yet it still affects many people. The conflict becomes obvious, and on several levels. For some, it is business versus spirituality, for others it is business or spirituality. Now, if you want to release business to focus on your spirituality, very good, but you still have to create income to house, feed and clothe your family. If you are a loner, with no responsibility except to yourself, then the options are enormous, but the family person has others to consider.

LIVING IT

Have your own business by all means, or work for a living in the usual way, but do not let work and money be your overriding focus. There are many stories of people no longer living who died immensely wealthy, yet unfulfilled, unhappy, and craving more wealth. An unfulfilled life, what a sad movie to continue with. Remember, this is your life-movie, so make it a happy one. By expressing your spiritual values in the business deals you do, or by focussing on the positive values in all the people you work with, you are combining your spirituality with your work. Until you are able to live and express your spirituality in the everyday workplace, your spirituality has no meaning. Spirituality is not some set of abstract, or conceptual esoteric knowledge held inside you, knowledge that makes you more spiritual; it is living your spiritual knowledge, fully and freely expressing it in every moment of your life. This is the place of true prosperity.

SUMMARY

As you speak and think, so you create your life. Let go forever of the far too familiar words, "I can't afford," replacing them with a hearty, "Plenty more money where this comes from." Trade in the feeling of loss and lack that goes with the former words, feeling the gain and zest that goes with the latter. But more than anything, the former will create and maintain that 'can't afford' reality, while the latter will create and maintain a flow of opportunity and income that will continually surprise you. As the new reality of plenty begins to work its magic in your life, you will realize that you are the magician. And this is a great feeling. Your emotions will become part of your new creative reality, working for you, rather than appearing to work against you. Remember, you fashion your life-movie with your thoughts, actions, and emotions. Combined - and they always are - your thoughts and emotions will create any reality that you focus on, and fully live. Make it a focus that you truly want. One that will support you in being a person of true prosperity.

I have learned that life is
always guiding and teaching
us. You can either go with
this, following the intuitive
prompting of your heart, or you
can resist, seeing the lessons as
a form of adversity, convinced
that life is against you.

4 A SUPPORTIVE FOCUS

SHATTERED DREAMS

In all the mishmash of our daily focus, by far the most common focus is fear. A good many years ago - in the days when even reading this book would have been a serious challenge for me! - I was a dairy farmer in Tasmania, the beautiful island state of Australia. With my wife Treenie, and two children, we emigrated from the U.K. in 1964. Despite knowing nothing about it, my plan was to be a 'beef baron.' In my idealistic fantasy I would own a lot of land, have a great herd of cattle, and manage everything without too much work. To this end, we bought a small beef cattle farm on the foothills of Mt. Arthur - I was prepared to grow bigger as we progressed - and so began a new way of life. Within a year reality stepped in, a grim reality that shattered my dreams. Just as effectively as a swarm of locusts, a plague of army-worm caterpillars wiped us out. In waves, they marched through the whole district, decimating our pasture. They died in such numbers in our water holes that the living caterpillars could crawl over the water on the bodies of the dead. When our cattle drank this putrid water, they sickened, and died. Sick and weak, the putrid water had a devastating effect on them, and veterinary assistance could do little to help. Between poisonous water and a merciful bullet, we lost most of our cattle.

SOUL BUILDING

This was my grim introduction to farming in Australia. For economic survival I was forced into dairy farming, not something that I wanted. It took me eight weeks to learn that I detested the daily milking routine, and eight more years before I could get out of it. You may think, why not sell out? Having had to borrow the money, we had just bought our cows and had the dairy herd up and running, when we entered into three years of what was to be the worst drought of the century for Tasmania. This was followed by a three-year rural recession, aggravated by a city boom. Ten-month-old vealer beef prices fell from Aus$350 average to Aus$8, if you could even sell them. Milk for cheese was at an all time low. Selling your farm during those times was no more than a dream. Who would buy into what we were experiencing?

Farmer deaths from heart attack and suicide were

escalating. The situation was described as soul destroying, and at the time I agreed, but as I look back I realize that for me, it had the opposite effect. Under that hardship, I grew mentally, emotionally, and spiritually. I grew in self-esteem and self-worth, finding unsuspected capacities.

FEAR OF FAILURE

I had big lessons to learn. Most importantly, I learned that it was fear who cracked the whip driving me to greater efforts. Pure fear. I would like to say that it was love for my family, or some other more enlightened reason, but it was fear. Based in low self-esteem, I was terrified of failure. Of course, I only had to explore my childhood - those formative years - and the reasons were all there. Does fear crack the whip that drives you? Do you do the work that you do because you fear what might happen if you quit? Do you *really* like the work you do? Is Friday your favourite day of the week? I smile at that last question. Milking cows was an 'everyday' affair! You may not want to face those questions. You may be afraid of what they bring up. You have been taught that financial security is paramount. But at what price? I have learned that life is always guiding and teaching us. You can either go with this, following the intuitive prompting of your heart, or you can resist, seeing the lessons as a form of adversity, convinced that life is against you.

LIFE REFLECTS

Do you believe that life is supportive of you, or resists all your efforts? This is very important, because your life will be a reflection of your beliefs.

During my twelve years on the farm in Tasmania, there was a time when my mother- and father-in-law paid for us - now with four children - to all go back for a visit to them in England. This was at the end of our eight years of milking. We had bred our way back into beef cattle, crossing our hundred Friesian dairy cows with Hereford beef bulls. I made care-taking arrangements with a nearby farmer friend to manage our farm during the six-week absence, and for a retired couple to live in and look after the house and pets. In high spirits, away we went. One night I had a dream. I dreamt that our wonderful, harmless Great Dane, Tandi, had been shot. The same night, Treenie dreamt that we had dead cows everywhere. When we arrived home, we learned that Len, the elderly retired husband, had died from a heart attack, that Tandi had been shot and killed, and that due to unforeseen circumstances we had twenty-six cattle dead from bracken poisoning. We were devastated.

However, one great undeniable reality was forced upon me; we did not own the farm, the farm owned us. Our life was determined by the farm, not by us. That shocked me.

LETTING GO

I used to declare loud and firm that I would die on the farm. Under constant financial pressure, I would state that this farm is mine, and nothing can take it from me. That was before our U.K. holiday! Strongly supported by my upbringing, I had always believed that to sell my farm indicated that I had failed. I had to let that belief go. I had to learn that life is about flexibility and adaptability, not stick, stay, and self-destruct. I had to learn that there are times when you dig in your heels, make more effort and persevere, and times when you let go, opening to the new, and moving with life. And I had to learn which was applicable!

Let us look at all this. First, does fear crack the whip that keeps you doing what you do, to not only earn a living, but your whole lifestyle and way of thinking? If you are fear based, then you have to make big changes. Fear will offer you a life of denial, of sacrifice, of inner turmoil and overall suffering. I know, I've been there. Not only that, you are deeply imprinting fear into your life-movie, meaning, there is more to come! Fear will never allow you to experience true prosperity. Fear will always deny abundance. The best you can hope for is temporary wealth. Physically, mentally and emotionally, you will pay the price.

LOOK AT YOUR FEARS

Obviously, there is a better way. First you need to face the question, does fear dominate your life? And fear comes in many disguises. Again, you need to do some honest inner appraisal. Are you fear motivated? Fear of failure, fear of parental disapproval, fear of peer group criticism, fear of not being good enough, financial fears, fear of life. The list is long. I faced my fears for many years, moving from farming into other ways of living that exposed even more inner fears. During this period I learned that it is okay to have fear, to be fearful, but it is not okay to let those fears determine the way you live. This is not the easiest lesson to learn, but a lesson that every person needs to face and embrace.

Be honest with yourself, and be gentle. Acknowledging your inner fears is a big step. Even better, share what you find with your partner, or a close friend. Tell them that you have just realised that your life is a journey of self-discovery, and you need to share some of it to make it more real for you. Sharing your inner fears takes courage, even just acknowledging them to yourself takes courage. And with courage, you can defeat fear. Or, maybe I should rephrase that, and explain it. We need to deal with fear honestly, not maintain a lie.

A POWERFUL ILLUSION

Fear is an illusion. It is not real. It is not something you can defeat. Fear is a self-created belief, or set of beliefs. Fear is a conditioning, a habit, a reaction based in the past. Someone in the U.S.A. with great insight wrote that FEAR is False Evidence Appearing Real. That is brilliant. It is always false. Fear is never based in Truth; it is based in and supported by illusion. Fear is you attacking yourself with your thinking. Fear is you imagining the worst. Imagining and thinking the worst, the most negative, over a long period of time creates a field of fear/energy that lives with and within you, its source. Living within this fear/energy you automatically react fearfully to the triggers that affect you. Not nice! So when I said you need to defeat fear, you cannot defeat it by opposing it. To oppose illusion is to strengthen it by giving it more credibility. You simply reinforce it. You have to see fear for what it is, and make the choices that most honour you, not your fear. Living from a foundation of fear does not honour you, and you are definitely worthy of honour.

The power of passion

Acknowledge your fear, but live from your courage. You are powerful, but you have to give yourself evidence of that courage to empower it. If you have a job you hate, then you need to either change your attitude to it, or you need to find employment that suits you. When work is daily punishment it sends very negative messages into your psyche. This is not the way of true prosperity. You need to find employment where you are at least reasonably happy at work, preferably happy and fulfilled. Listening to the radio recently, I heard a man talking about his life. He was a real estate agent, and absolutely loved his work. He had a passion for what he did, meeting people and meeting their needs.

There is power in your passion. I have said that you are powerful, but this power has to find the trigger that allows it expression. Passion is a trigger. Enthusiasm is another. To be enthusiastic about your work, relationships, life, has the quality of attraction. You not only attract people, but you attract solutions to problems that may occur. With passion and enthusiasm you are putting very positive messages into your surrounding field of energy. An old friend of mine is the anchor man for a television show, *Gardening Australia*. Peter's unbounded enthusiasm and passion for plants and gardening is the greatest attraction of the program. His enthusiasm is like a people magnet, inspiring and uplifting. He loves what he is doing. His unbridled enthusiasm is the reason he has the key job of anchor man.

MANY VARIABLES

I also am very enthusiastic about what I do. I love public speaking and writing books. I get enormous pleasure from inspiring people, and influencing their lives for the better. I, too, have a passion for my garden and keeping fish. Everything I do reflects my love of life, but it was not always like this. I mention focus a lot, because your every moment is spent with some sort of focus, whether muddled, angry, cynical, hostile, fearful, anxious, pessimistic, all negative, or, on the brighter side, with clarity, good cheer, openness, gentleness, courage, trust, optimism, all positive. All these are choices. I repeat, the negatives are automatic, while the positives have to be chosen. Each is a focus, the framework of attracting a similar energy into your life. So pessimism attracts more reasons to be pessimistic, while optimism attracts ever more to be optimistic about. Obviously, you need a supportive focus. You need to work in employment, or own a business, where you feel happy and worthwhile. This attracts qualities into your life that you are going to enjoy. Once you learn to give to yourself in this way, it escalates. Life will also give to you in ways that will surprise you.

Subconscious focus

Focus is not something that many people think about as having any value. It is disregarded, yet never inactive. I repeat, our thoughts and spoken words are an ever-ongoing focus. In fact, it becomes a subconscious focus. If you are working in an office environment or situation that is not to your liking, within your mind there will be a continuous stream of subconscious negative chatter. This chatter will be disparaging about life, your chances in life, how you are not good enough, while replaying all the negatives you heard spoken about you when you were a child. It all gets replayed on a deep subliminal level - and that is your focus for the day! Not nice. It means that every day will be a repeat - more of the same. True prosperity comes from a true prosperity focus. Any supportive focus will set the ball rolling in the right direction, but you have to release a self-destructive focus.

SEXUAL FOCUS

As a public speaker, I get a lot of e-mail. Since my book *The Magic Formula* was published a lot of men have shared their troubles with me. Often I get an e-mail from a man who is homosexual, and the contents are invariably filled with self-hate and shame. Why? There is no crime involved, and even if it is not your sexual preference, it is what you have. While I can understand the reasons for the men to have the self-loathing, I am certain that if they were heterosexual they would still find other reasons for self-hate. Focus! This is how it works. A lifetime - one frame of your life-movie - focus of self-loathing creates and attracts reasons to continue that loathing. If you spent a lifetime loathing another person's homosexuality, your focus has been hate and homosexuality. All this is attracted by your focus into your field of creative energy - you. Guess what is waiting in the next frame of your life-movie? True prosperity begins with true acceptance of yourself. It matters not what your sexuality is, it is not a block to your well-being unless you make it a block. Any sexual therapist will tell you that heterosexual people have just as many sexual hang-ups as do homosexuals. Do not let your sexuality be a reason for self-hatred or shame. The focus creates repercussions that will pursue you for a long time. Be accepting of yourself.

SUICIDAL DESPAIR

Several of the e-mails I get about their homosexuality speak of the men's suicidal feelings. Self-hate and despair is only a step away from suicide. And suicide is a terrible and tragic focus to maintain. Self-hate and despair blindly see suicide as a way of killing self, a way out of a situation they cannot deal with. Hate and despair cannot see that it does not work, that it has no reality. You can kill a body, but self continues. Suicide can become a self-repeating loop. Hate and despair create the false illusion of a solution that proves to be no solution at all. All this is based in seeing self in a judgmental and fragmented way.

Instead of the usual way of seeing life and self as beginning and ending, look at it as a continuous whole. You cannot judge a continuous whole, it would be utterly meaningless. You are here to experience life; homosexuality is an experience just as heterosexuality is an experience. Neither should be judged as good or bad, right or wrong. Release the judgment and self-criticism and you release self-hate and despair. You do not fight or oppose these negative expressions, but from a platform of Truth, you release them.

Avoid gossip

Focus. It is always with you. If you are a person who likes to gossip about others in a negative way, be aware that your words are taking meaning and shape in your life. To my surprise, I heard a therapist on the radio recently talking of the virtues of gossip. She said how good it was for talking 'it' out and relieving inner tension. If, as I assume, 'it' is your troubles or problems, then talking it out is indeed good therapy, but this is not the meaning of gossip. Gossip means to indulge in idle and meaningless talk. Having a chat with friends over a cup of coffee can be very recreational, but please, avoid gossip. Avoid ever talking about life or people in a disparaging or negative way, because your words are creating your focus for your life - and you deserve better. Meaningless gossip creates a meaningless focus creating a meaningless life - and so it continues.

To say, or not to say?

When people do gather, either at the coffee table or at parties, the quality of conversation generally takes a sharp downward turn for the worse. I confess, in the past I have listened to myself talking words that were utterly meaningless to me, simply to hold up my end of the conversation. I no longer do that. I either avoid the party, or avoid the idle chatter of a group. One on one can be meaningful, insightful, and very helpful. Other people I have mentioned this to mostly claim the same experience. "I don't know why I do it," one acquaintance grumbled to me while we were at a party. "Perhaps it's because social acceptance is more important to you than being true to yourself," I suggested. He gave me a hard look, and walked away. Obviously I was right! But that is the crunch. If you live true to your higher qualities, your superficial social life will disintegrate. It is worth the price, what is left will be of quality and virtue. As a focus, a social butterfly leaves a lot to be desired. Life does not give you time out for a party, it is all included in focus and attraction, magnetising situations into your life. Of course, when it is unpleasant, you tend to blame life, other people, or the ever reliable standby, the govern-ment! You seldom want to accept that as your life is now, you created it; you are the script writer, the film maker.

Party time

Party by all means, have fun. Fun and laughter create wonderful chemical cocktails in your brain that do far more for your true prosperity than the cocktails in the glass. But be true to yourself in your words and actions. Even alcohol is a focus! When alcohol is used with respect and discretion, it can add to the quality of your life, but as soon as disregard creeps in, and alcohol becomes a support, you are in trouble. Alcohol will not support you. It will destroy, but never support you. A glass of red wine at the appropriate time, either alone or with good company, can be very positive, but when that glass becomes a need, your focus is shifting from an independent self, to a dependency on alcohol.

If you are with the family, or in a group having an evening meal, and conversation turns to blaming the government, or the multinationals, or terrorism, or the state of the world, just realize that you are back into judgment and blame. No matter how well-founded or re-searched the words, no matter that the media may have offered proof of governmental indiscretion, the energies of blame, hostility and resentment are blending in with the energy of self. It will go home with you, and linger. It will join with other subconscious blame and resentment, and it will add to your subliminal background murmur of negativity . That party conversation of blame will weave blame into the threads of your life.

Higher and lighter

If it was a one-off situation, the effect will be mini-mal, if it is a fairly regular occurrence, then the effects are already in your life. Speaking your highest truth at a party is not likely to win you many friends, unless the people at the party are more aware; people of a higher, finer consciousness. And these parties do happen, I have been to several. So often the overriding factor in party conversation is the need of social approval. If you speak similar words as other people to express similar views, and yet you know these are words and values that are not true to you, or your reality, you are creating a focus that will eventually devalue you. Even if you oppose the common thinking, speaking words of attack and scorning their views, you are still the loser. You are all expressing the same energy.

The aftermath of the party offers an opportunity to rethink your life and its direction. If the overriding opinions of current friends are not reflecting your views on life, then you need to gently let some of those relationships fade out, making new friendships with more compatible and uplifting people.

SUMMARY

True prosperity requires a focus on the abundance of life. Your focus is part of the aperture through which life flows, remembering that you are the creator of all this. If true prosperity is desirable for you, then you have to accept responsibility for your life. You need to release all blame, either of yourself or other people. Blame is a rotten focus.

In everyday life you have to choose your focus, this takes persistence and awareness. Mix with people whom you admire and respect, both for their attitudes and for their lifestyle. Do not attempt to copy them, just allow the stimulus of positive and/or uplifting thoughts to take you in a direction that you really want to go. This is not about wealth, or deliberately mixing with the wealthy; it is about mixing with people of awareness, people who leave you 'feeling good'. If you need to be inspired - and everyone does - then you mix with inspiring and positive people. In this way you create a focus that will consistently honour you. It will place you on the path of true prosperity.

*A*ppreciation begins with what you now have, and with the person you are, right now.

5 AN ATTITUDE OF GRATITUDE

GROWING UP

I grew up in middle-class England. My family as a whole was comparatively wealthy in those days and, as with most children, I took this pretty much for granted. I am certain that today's kids are far more financially demanding than in my generation. Without television and mass advertising I had no idea of what was available, and my needs reflected this. A bicycle was both a necessary form of transport and an enjoyable freedom machine; it was all that I really wanted or needed. I have an academically brilliant brother who is three years older than me. He, therefore, set the academic standards for both of us. While he enjoyed school, thriving under the intellectual stimulus, my situation was very different. I loathed school. I hated everything about it. The only redeeming factor was that I learned to read at school. Once I discovered books, I found a new and vastly more sympathetic world. From the age of six I have read prolifically, feeding and enriching my imagination. Almost all my reading has been, and still is, for the enrichment of my imagination. I get my knowledge from life. For me, knowledge is not about facts from books, it is about harvesting the rich experiences of life. When you have read this book you will have the concepts and inspiration gained from some of my knowledge. Not until you live it, bringing it into your life and experiencing it, will you have the actual knowledge.

PRIVATE SCHOOL

I had to endure ten years of private school. Not wishing to live in his shadow, I made sure that I failed the exam that would have taken me to my brother's school. My school had teachers with all the academic qualifications, but few of the humane qualities. I am sure none of them liked children! I rebelled from the very beginning, endlessly going from one mishap to the next. I was thrashed in front of the whole school assembly four times in the ten years, enduring many a private caning. It just made things worse. To survive, I learned to lie and cheat, not that I am proud of it. However, to my credit, when I left school a month before my fifteenth birthday, I also left behind my lies and cheating. I left school with the impression that I was intellectually incapable, and with very low self-esteem. When I look back for any redeeming qualities in that now extinct school, there were very few; camaraderie and friendships with other kids, little else. Even our sport training was hackneyed and woefully inadequate. All this under the eagle eye of a truly eccentric headmistress. And do you know . . . it was perfect! It was the foundation that set up the dynamic and potent brew that was to prompt and spur me in the directions that led to me being who I am today.

CREATIVE CONNECTIONS

It took forty-nine years before I could look back with gratitude. Let me offer here another Principle of Truth: Nothing in life ever works against you! I can imagine how many people will disagree with that. So what do I mean? I mean that every incident in your life - and I mean *every* - no matter how insignificant or enormous, no matter how positive or negative, all leads to the next incident, each drawing from your inner reserves those qualities needed to help you deal with your issues and progress. Like varying beads on a necklace, all are part of the whole, each holding its own meaning and place in the overall movie of Self. Every experience that we generally label as bad offers you the opportunity to 'let go' and grow. The bad experience is not working against you. You either nourish your resentments and blame, or you feed your more positive qualities. Remembering also, that you are the writer of that movie, you create many challenging situations designed primarily for soul growth. The fact that you are seldom aware of this is simply because very few people are consciously focussed on, or aware of their soul growth. We are easily distracted, and distractions abound. Every bead on that necklace leads to, and compliments the final product.

SOUL JOURNEY

In this case, you are the final product. Or, to be more accurate for us as human Beings, there is no finality, no ending, just higher and finer stages in the evolution of a soul. And this is what you truly are about. Not financial wealth, not acquisition, but growing and developing the finest human Being that you can be. This is the realm of true prosperity. And you can do this with all the material wealth that you need, all the financial assets.

If you focus on your soul growth during the wheeling and dealing of your business life, it will always work for you, no matter how adverse it may seem in the short term view. If, however, your focus is entirely on material acquisition and financial gain, then despite the illusions of wealth and success, in the long term you are creating more hurdles to overcome. You are a soul on a journey, and a denial of this Truth equates as the denial of self.

WHOLISTIC MOVIE

This is where you come to the attitude of gratitude. I now look back on my life with genuine gratitude. Unknowingly, I chose the school I went to, and I chose the teachers. After all, I am the creator of my life-movie. Each new frame in your life-movie begins as soon as you are born. Actually, to be really accurate, the movie is wholistic, meaning that the whole 'Continuity of Self' movie, every frame, is all being created simultaneously, simply because all time occupies the same space. But for the purpose of this book, I choose to refer to the moment of your birth as beginning the creation of each new frame. In choosing my school and teachers, my soul self knew exactly what I needed to develop certain hidden qualities. The fact that those qualities only began to emerge around my thirty-fifth year is an indication of my subconscious resistance to inner growth and change.

MATRIARCHAL FEAR

I now appreciate the brilliant, eccentric, Mrs. Livingstone Taylor, my headmistress. Her continual hard and angry slaps around my head helped to reinforce the matriarchal fears that I did not know I had. My mother's occasional, frustrated and angry use of the cane helped me in later years to see that I brought a problem into this frame of the movie that had been with me for a long time. Add to this home brew my grandmother's dominating nature, and it becomes obvious that I chose to be born into such impatient matriarchal dominance.

I now appreciate the time when, in my early forties, I walked into a little coffee shop and saw a certain woman sitting at a table with some friends. Before I was even aware of doing it, I found myself tiptoeing backwards out of the coffee shop, hoping that she would not see me. Why? Because she epitomised everything matriarchal in a woman that frightened me. Although I did not know it at the time, it was to be a pivotal moment for me.

FACING THAT FEAR

Only a few months later I had to confront this woman on a certain issue. I chose to do this. I had become aware of my matriarchal fear. I chose it because the coffee shop situation clearly showed me how terrified I was of her. I could have left the confrontation to another person who had no personal issues with her, but then I would have to face and live with my lack of courage. While I waited for her at our prearranged meeting, I could feel the sweat running down my spine. My hands were sweating, my face and forehead dripping, my stomach churning. She was late, allowing me plenty of time to be painfully aware of my bodily reactions, of my fear. I had no idea what to say to her. Normally very articulate, my thoughts blanked out. When she suddenly entered the room, I walked toward her and, without thought or predetermination, I became truly vulnerable to her. I dropped my customary defenses, and on sheer impulse I told her of my reaction to her presence in the coffee shop. And as I told her in complete openness, my whole body stopped sweating. I felt an incredible lightness sweeping through me, a sense of freedom utterly new to me. As I finished the story of telling her how frightened I was of her, I stopped and stared at her. Then I smiled. "Wow! I'm not frightened of you anymore."

I told her what I needed to say relating to our meeting, and she gave me her usual articulate, scathing, and cynical reply. She made it very clear that she intensely disliked me, treating me to the usual scorn and dismissal . . . and it did not hurt one little bit. I was cured.

LOOK BACK WITH GRATITUDE

Should I look back in anger and resentment to her, or with immense appreciation? Because she represented the peak of my matriarchal fear she gave me a 'forever' gift that no other women could possibly give me. Of course I am grateful. Although, in fact, she gave me nothing, it was that meeting with her that brought my matriarchal fears to a head. My gift came from using my courage and in becoming vulnerable to her, instead of my usual old act of defensive aggression. When I look back in life every person who seemed to give me a hard time was offering me future growth. Equally, those people who offered friendship and caring gave me a great gift, but without doubt it was the difficult ones, the people I did not like, who offered me the most inner growth and development.

Develop an attitude of gratitude. Become aware that the people who seem the most abrasive in your life are the ones who are polishing your rough edges. View them with a sense of appreciation, not resentment and resistance. Every person who rubs you the wrong way has something to offer you. Something that you need to release, or develop, as part of your inner growth toward true prosperity.

TAKING FOR GRANTED

I said in opening this chapter that I took pretty much everything for granted through the years of my youth. Unfortunately, this continued into my life. At twenty-one I married the love of my life, Treenie. Looking back, I realize that I even took her for granted. I took a happy marriage for granted. I even took myself for granted, with a casual and dismissive 'I am who I am' approach. It never occurred to me that the person I could become was a much greater, far wiser man. Taking self, other people, or fortune for granted is not a good way to live. It creates complacency and stagnation in your life, eventually building up to many hard lessons in appreciation. And I had a lot!

Soon after Treenie and I were married, my father built us a lovely house on the farm. We had a few blissful - taken for granted - years, before he developed cancer and died. He died without making his will and testament. Abruptly, the farming life in England that I had expected to inherit was in disarray. The winds of change were rippling my complacency. The final outcome was that I took my quarter share from the proceeds of the sale of the farm, and Treenie, our two boys and myself emigrated to Australia. We bought the hill farm, and I took it for granted that I would continue life as a farmer.

ONE OR THE OTHER

The army-worm caterpillars were the forerunners of the old, well-worn, but overlooked message of life; never take anything for granted. By the time the following long drought and rural recession had finished with me, my taking life for granted was in tatters. Only now was I ready to learn about appreciation. You have to realize that 'appreciation' and 'taking for granted' cannot both occupy the same space. You are living either one or the other.

It was not until I reached the time in my life when I had lost all my possessions; no farm, no money, no home of my own, just a continually loving and supportive wife, that I learned to truly appreciate Treenie. A lesson never forgotten. It was then that I saw through the 'taken for granted' trap, and saw Treenie for the incredible gift she truly was/is in my life. During the ten years of not owning our own home, and with the prospect of owning one fading year by year, I came to appreciate all that I had once had. And only then did I truly learn to give inner thanks for all that I had. What a dichotomy!

If you wait to receive before you begin to appreciate, you will wait a long time. Appreciation begins with what you now have, and with the person you are, right now. Begin with the qualities in yourself that you know are positive and noble. Begin with your capable body and health. Begin by waking each morning with a sense of gratitude that another day is here, and you are fit and well. Realize what a blessing it is to be able to walk, to be able to see from your eyes, and hear the world around you. For many, these things are impossible. Look around you and see what you have, and let that be your focus. When appreciation is your focus it attracts into your life more and more reasons for appreciation. A very positive step toward true prosperity. You cannot have true prosperity without a well-developed and well-used sense of appreciation. And use develops it!

COUNTING BLESSINGS

During our time of farming hardship in Tasmania, when the stress and pressure from unpaid bills and endlessly living with financial hardship became too much for us, Treenie and I would get into our old Land Rover and drive up to the highest point of our farm. With a lofty altitude of approximately 665 metres (2000 ft), we were high on a tree-covered shoulder of Mt. Arthur. From here, we could see over our whole farm. For a while we would just quietly stare at it, then looking at each other we would cuddle, and say, "Aren't we blessed. We have each other, and our love. We have four wonderful children, aren't we blessed. We have our health, and this beautiful farm, aren't we blessed. We have so much in our lives, aren't we blessed. What don't we have? We don't have enough cash."

We would laugh, and kiss, feeling uplifted. We could take a long time going through the list of what we did have, seeing how blessed we were, while a single sentence summed up what we did not have. It changed our whole perspective. Under the daily pressures the lack of money loomed huge and menacing, but when we took those precious moments to re-evaluate, the perspective became more realistic and encouraging.

A HAVE OR HAVE-NOT SITUATION

To this day, Treenie considers that as one of the major steps forward in our lives. I agree. Without us realizing it, we were invoking a powerful Principle; What you focus on is what you empower. Our focus was on our blessings, appreciation for what we had. There is an odd quotation in the Bible: "To those who have, it shall be given, from those who have not, it shall be taken." Odd because it seems so unjust, so unfair. However, a more enlightened view reveals the meaning very clearly. If you focus on what you have - as we did - life gives you more. If you focus on what you do not have - lack of - then life takes from you, and you have less. It reinforces what I repeatedly emphasise, you are the creator of your life-movie. You write the script, you determine both the cause and effect in your life.

Looking back, I now appreciate the hardship of those farming years. I worked from five o'clock in the morning until seven o'clock at night, plus all the late nights with the hay season and so many nights of helping a cow with her calving. That work load, along with the constant financial pressure, developed the inner strengths and character of who I am today. I respect and deeply appreciate who I am today, but what I have today, and who I am, is due to the sum of all the yesterdays. Everything that seemed to be against me when I struggled in life, was helping me to reach the place where life is no longer a struggle.

GO WITH THE FLOW

Life is like a flowing river. Instead of swimming against the flow as I used to, I now allow the river to carry me. Instead of having a preconceived destiny to which I adhere, and for which I struggle - ambition - I now trust the flow of life, knowing it will deliver me gracefully and in perfect timing at the place I am meant to be. Gratitude is part of that flow. When you develop such a gratitude for life, life just loves to delightfully surprise you and, in the way of serendipity, offers you many unexpected treats.

One of the important aspects of appreciation is about how you relate to life. And this means how you relate to yourself. Another Principle: Your relationship with self is your relationship with life. In other words, if you really do not like yourself, you do not enjoy life and living. You have no zest for life, no joy. Develop an attitude of gratitude. If you can learn to be happy with what you have, you will soon have more. Happiness is a vital ingredient in the true prosperity package. Never wait for life to give you more. If you wait for life, life will wait for you. Happiness comes from the inside out, not from the outside in. So many people need to learn that. If you wait for life to give you reasons to be happy, you will wait a long time, but if you are simply happy because you are alive and grateful for life, then life will abundantly offer you ever more reasons for happiness.

SCENE AND SCENERY

Life is . . . you first, then life. Do you get it? You set the scene, life will fill in the scenery. You cannot have the scenery first. That is not possible. By your attitude to life, you set the stage, you determine the props. Imagine what incredible scenery follows if you live with an inner appreciation of yourself and life. An appreciation of self is by far and away the most important. Why? Another Principle: There is nothing outside of Self. Nothing outside the field of energy of who you truly are. So if you appreciate self, you are appreciating life. You are holding hands with abundance. If you look outside of yourself, waiting for something to appreciate, you will still be waiting when you die. Dare to love self. Dare to respect and appreciate yourself. I say 'dare' because I know of people who, literally, dare not. Their religious indoctrination and negative conditioning against such a seemingly selfish act have made self-love almost impossible for them. That is a sad place to be.

MISFORTUNE OR FORTUNE?

Know that you are worthy of love. When you think of yourself with love and appreciation, love and appreciation flow into your life. Again, you have to take a long-term view of this. We have all read of loving, selfless people who have been burgled, had their house catch fire, or some other major misfortune. How easy to say, "There, you see, it simply proves life sucks!" If that is your attitude and focus, you will be right. But if, at a later time, you were to visit that person whose fortune turned against them, and talk with them, you would most probably learn that the incident held a time of major inner growth, when on a soul level they prospered enormously. True prosperity and abundance holds far more than the eye can easily see, or the mind can easily understand. Soul and self prosper together.

83

LITTLE IS BIG!

Treenie and I now own a beautiful large house with a glorious hectare of garden, much of which is filled with eucalyptus trees. In Australia, we call it bush! During the ten years when we rented a house and such bounty seemed impossible, I learned to appreciate the little things in life. I learned that the 'little' things are 'big' - in disguise. It is all relative.

Now, I walk around our magnificent garden, admiring the plants and looking at the house - our home - and my sense of appreciation is often so overwhelming that I have tears in my eyes. It hits my emotional buttons. I no longer take ownership for granted. I find the joy of life in the moment, in living, and in my soul growth. When I look back at my life, I cannot see a moment of pain or adversity that was not advantage in disguise.

SUMMARY

When you treat yourself as though you are a king or queen, then life will fill in all the entitlements. This will not necessarily be as gifts, but as opportunities. When you are open to life, then life will offer you new openings. When you live your life each day as if it is a special occasion, life will present extra special occasions of wonder and joy. Appreciation is a key to true prosperity. Look at yourself and your life, and list all the things that you can deeply appreciate. Appreciation does not begin with what you own, or have, it begins with who you are, and the many blessings in your life. Develop a gratitude attitude, where you take notice of everything in your life for which you can be grateful. You will find that the list steadily gets longer, that as your self-appreciation grows, so will your friendships and relationships. You are the movie maker, write a script of appreciation and gratitude into your life.

When you acknowledge that you are a spiritual Being of infinite worth, then you have a strong and true foundation on which to build true prosperity.

6 THINKING TRUE PROSPERITY

ABOUT SECURITY

Without a doubt, most people do not think prosperity. The most common pattern of thinking in this money-driven age is poverty thinking. "I can't afford," typifies this perfectly. Obviously, you cannot have true prosperity while thoughts of poverty echo through your mind and psyche.

It is when you are most filled with self-doubt that your parents' beliefs and teachings come through at their strongest. My father held very strong views about life. Some were wise, worth taking on board, but others were his bitter experiences externalised. One of his most repeated statements went like this; "Security, my son, is bricks and mortar, land, or money in the bank." And for many years I considered it a gem. Surely it would be impossible to be insecure if you owned houses, land, or had money. Today, I look on that as false security, hollow and empty. I cannot imagine how many people build their lives on that premise. And die still believing it, unwilling or unable to see through its temporary and transient illusions.

IN SEARCH OF A DREAM

When Treenie and I sold our farm in Tasmania, we had been through a lot of inner growth and change. We both had a dream that we wanted to pursue; to join or begin an intentional community of people with a daily focus of body, mind, and spirit. This did eventuate and, with a few other people, we created the community, but as a dream for a community of people to focus on, and live this way, it remained an unrealised dream. I had no idea of the difficulties involved for a community of people to combine idealism with realism! It was always the imbalance of either one or the other. However, on a personal level, Treenie and I lived in that community situation for four years, then, having found the nucleus of what we were looking for within ourselves, we moved out, living again as a family.

Let me pick up the story where we were traveling around Australia, having just left Tasmania. We had sold the farm, paid our debts, bought a Nissan E-20 van, which I fitted with seats, and we towed a small 4 metre x 2 meter caravan (trailer). This also sums up most of our worldly possessions. With our four children, we were off on an adventure. On the very first day, as we set off on our odyssey, I felt the first stirrings of fear. I had not expected that. I had unburdened myself of the farm debt. I was free to travel, beginning a new life of freedom with Treenie, with no strings attached. Or so I thought!

INSECURE AND DISILLUSIONED

It did not happen that way. Eager anticipation and expectations were crushed more each day that passed. I was crushed! Where was my financial freedom? Where was the daily excitement of new hopes, new opportunities? "Security is bricks and mortar, land, or money in the bank," buzzed around in my mind like an angry wasp. The attached string was made of heavy chain! I had no security. Just one small piece of land we could not sell. No house, and so little in the bank that every time we filled the Nissan with petrol - and it was constant - I sweated at the thought of our rapidly receding bank account. Even worse, I was alone with my fear. Treenie tried to talk me out of it, while I tried to talk her into it. We both failed! For the first time I truly got in touch with my deep-seated insecurity.

That experience sticks in my memory like a burr. I was involved in an unrecognised, unwanted, cycle of growth. All I ever had to do was release the illusion of material security, and be open to learning that the only security is in Self, in knowing who you are. But I had no knowledge of this. I grew up in an era when a husband and father was totally responsible for his wife and children. It is generally accepted nowadays that this is a shared responsibility, as it was/is for us, but my conditioning held no regard for reality. 'I am responsible, I am a failure'; those were the thoughts, spurred by my insecurity, that continually whipped me.

THE SECURITY OF NO-SECURITY!

Your only true security is within you. You can neither coerce an awareness of it, nor can you manipulate circumstances to force the inner experience of it. Meet your material needs by all means, and even feel safe and secure in home ownership, or from a high income - but never believe that this will alleviate your deeper insecurities. A high income and/or property ownership certainly is 'financial' security, that is not in question, but all financial insecurity simply reflects from other, deep-seated insecurities. Buried in your subconscious, these insecurities generally come from earlier frames of your life-movie.

The security that you need to develop is in being truly secure within yourself. A security that does not depend on outside support. A security that, if you lost everything, will still stabilise and support you. A security built in Truth, in knowing that life is supportive of you, even in your darkest moments, even in your greatest loss, even in your pain and despair. How do you find such inner security? Living the Principles outlined within this book will give you such security. Taking the Principles beyond just words and concepts into a living reality. An inner security that is based in self is all part of your true prosperity.

THE UPS AND DOWNS

Consider this story about a highflyer on about half-a-million dollars a year. He owned a large and luxurious home, had a lovely wife and children, and they lived expensively. He was in his late forties, very competent in the multinational company he worked for. One day, out of the blue, he was made redundant. Apparently, he was 'too' ambitious, and behind his back the knives had been sharpened, then used with devastating effect. He struggled to persuade the other directors to rescind the decision, fighting bitterly for his survival. He failed.

To cut a fairly long story short, this man was plunged from the pinnacle of his profession into sudden unemployment. He was confident that he could get work with rival businesses, but after months of effort, the doors remained closed to him. He went from a seemingly confident, capable man to suicidal within eighteen months. All his security was in the prestige of his work position, his high income, and in his property value. It took only a further eighteen months for his marriage to fail, his wife leaving with the children. His property was sold, but he found that despite his previous high income, his lifestyle had surpassed it. With his ex-wife's financial claims and their debts paid, he came out of it with about one hundred thousand dollars.

MISMANAGEMENT

One hundred thousand dollars. For most people that is a lot of money. But not for this man. He was now a shattered human wreck of insecurity. Instead of seeing how much he still had, he focussed on, and continually moaned about, how much he had lost. Having been used to alcohol, he turned to drink as a support for his woes - and his woes multiplied. The final outcome saw him reduced to a penniless alcoholic, blaming, blaming, blaming.

Not such an unusual story, but it highlights the serious mismanagement of the man himself. He could manage his business life and his family life, and while his dependency on money was met, all seemed okay, but when crisis came, he was unable to manage himself.

The whole crux of true prosperity is self-management. Business management is nowhere near as important as self-management. Why is this so neglected? To me, it seems so obvious that if you are capable and competent in self-management, then it must flow into whatever you do for financial income. Equally obvious, is that the reverse of this does not bring about a beneficial outcome.

A DIFFERENT VIEW

This unfortunate man could have had a very different life-movie. After all, he made it. The common saying, "life is what you make it," has far more truth than most people realise. Without any doubt, beneath his income and lifestyle his personal insecurities simmered and festered. In his subconscious mind, they became a focus. Beneath the veneer of success, wealth, and ownership, year by year he was creating and maintaining a focus on his insecurities. And what we focus on is what we empower and attract.

Let me give you a different view of this man and his tragic story. He, like all of us, is on this planet for soul growth. No matter how life may appear, this is your first and foremost purpose of being. You may discard this for many frames of your life-movie, but eventually it has to be faced. In fact, the longer time spent ignoring the inner voice, delaying the needs of the soul, the greater the impact when it finally arises. So, within this man was a need to face the inner issues of his long-term insecurity. How do you do that? On a soul level you create a crisis that is designed to make you face, head-on, what you have avoided for a long, long time. We could say that he handled it badly, and there is some short-term truth in this, he could have done much better, but remember, a person's insecurities have their own agenda, their own voice, and fear speaks screamingly loud. You and I both know this!

HUMAN WORTH

Equally, however, it could have been suppressed for another frame of his life-movie and he could have continued in his facade as a 'successful' man. He could have lived the illusion of financial security being his true security for another lifetime, but he did not. However badly he mismanaged himself, the issue is now exposed in his life-movie. Exposed, it will eventually be dealt with. The when and where is not important. What matters is that his insecurity is no longer buried under self-deceit. What is important is that he will have to face a simple reality; no matter what a person's status is in life, they have immense value purely as a human Being. When you acknowledge that you are a spiritual Being of infinite worth, then you have a strong and true foundation on which to build true prosperity.

In the man's story, I do not see either failure or success. I see that where he had become stagnant and unmoving under the weight of his illusion, there is now spiritual movement. The fact that his life appears to be totally messed up is simply based in how other people think that it should be. People would see his life as going wrong. It is neither going wrong or right, he is now growing, and adversity causes good growth.

REDEFINING LIFE

Indeed, adversity does cause good growth, and it seems the way of most of humanity. I certainly grew through adversity, and from adversity came the true prosperity that I now enjoy. *But it does not have to be that way.* It is not the way of wisdom. You can grow far less painfully by finding harmony within life, moving through life with confidence and trust. This can bring about very powerful growth, especially when life is fully supportive. Life supports true reality, not the illusions. Illusions are, in fact, lifeless.

I suggest that you spend some time redefining your life. What are your goals? Do they embrace the long-term wholistic self, or are they based in short-term wealth? What does the reality of life mean for you? Are you living with, and supporting illusions? Supporting the illusions of life is a poor deal, because the illusions will not support you.

There are no rights or wrongs in any of this, but if you view your stay in life as temporary - one life and that is it! - then your goals will almost certainly be for the quick haul. However worthwhile they may seem, they will not serve you as well as if you embrace the wholistic picture. Redefine your desires. Make the decisions that assist you in letting go of attachments, of wanting this and that. A few wants are okay, that is part of life, but do not let your wants outstrip your ability to easily supply them. It is a simple fact that desires create more to desire. The more you have, the more you want. This is well enough known, but for most people it remains as words, rather than as realised reality.

THE AUSSIE BATTLER

I have heard many reasons for a person's financial struggle. Some almost bizarre. Many people are literally addicted to struggle. Who needs that, you might think, but it is far more common than you may realise. The Australian psyche is fairly well-saturated in it. I like the people of Oz, they are big-hearted, easy-going and friendly; a great nation of wonderful, very generous people. But somewhere in the Oz psyche a gremlin was established. It even has a term to define it; the Aussie battler. As a generalisation, the Aussies love a battler - but only for as long as they keep battling. If the battler becomes a winner, then the love affair comes to an end. Even the media promotes this, albeit perhaps unwittingly. A man - an entrepreneur perhaps - battles his way along in life gathering a fair bit of supportive media coverage. Or it may be a woman in politics who has struggled from obscurity in the back-benches of government, to being a front-bencher, a major player. They each become a winner, well-known, and regularly documented in the newspapers and television. Now, the media becomes hostile. No longer focused on the positive qualities of the people concerned, they mostly look for the negatives that can be reported. They look for the dirt.

EXPOSED

The repercussions of this are nasty. And let us be clear, it is not only Oz with a cynical negative press. With the media now running against them, the hypothetical entrepreneur or politician have only to make one slip, a single error, one humanly stupid move - and the media pounces. Then we read of the big 'expose.' Under the media microscope, a lifetime of big or little errors are paraded before the public. They are publicly humiliated and disgraced. After that, all press coverage is fronted with the words, the 'failed . . . !' For the people of the nation - all nations - this perpetuates and maintains the negative focus so common today.

Redefine your focus. If you are a person whose focus is other people's struggles, you are creating struggle in your own life. Not a good way for true prosperity. Do you read the Daily Negative newspaper before going to work each day? Or do you watch it on television? Redefine your focus. What you constantly feed into your psyche is what will eventually appear in your life. If it is based in the negative media, be sure that you will not like it.

IMPROVING HIMSELF

One man told me how, coming from a factory worker background, he managed to save his money, use it well, and improve the quality of his, and his family's life. He eventually bought himself a small farm, doing reasonably well as a family provider. He was quietly proud of this, as well he might be. The price he paid was to be ostracised by his workmates and even his friends. They considered that he should accept his 'lot in life,' and should not seek to 'better' himself. Eventually he moved from the area, putting all that behind him, but he was unable to leave behind the years of spite, scorn, and all the negative criticism. That had moved into him, becoming part of the subconscious murmur that can so easily sabotage the quality of a person's life. All this precipitated heart problems in him.

We talked about this, but he was more able to talk bitterly about it than listen to ways to remedy it. His focus had become his bitterness against the people of his past. He did not realise that he was the one harvesting his own bitterness. As I told him, bitterness is like an acid, it destroys its own container first. He clearly had a need to redefine his focus.

COMPARISONS

It never ceases to amaze me how many people compare themselves with others. One of our champion Olympic swimmers recently said how crazy it was for regular people to compare themselves with the top-class dedicated athletes. He was absolutely right. There is no basis for comparison, it simply leads to low self-esteem.

I have spoken to really beautiful women who

genuinely believe that they are unattractive. When I have asked them how they have come to such an incredible belief, they often talk of the film star, or model, with whom they compare themselves. I ask them if they know that science has stated that every snowflake is unique. This is well-documented, and generally they have heard of this. Then I ask them if they think that every human Being is unique. Again, they mostly concede that this is so.

"Tell me then, how do you make a comparison with uniqueness?" I ask. "Unique means a one-off, no other like it, without equal. If you are without equal, how can you compare, when in Truth, you are beyond comparison? It makes no sense."

As if sense makes any difference where people are concerned! However, I have never yet received an adequate answer. There is none! All they do is pick a model or star who does not have the same perceived flaws, or imperfections, that they perceive in themselves. Guess what their focus is!

Never compare yourself with anybody. Men, particularly, do not compare yourself with your father, either for better or worse. You are unique, not a revised version of an older model. Ladies, never compare yourselves with any glamorous star, celebrate your uniqueness. Comparison leads to self-pity, despair, to supporting false beliefs and utterly unrealistic expectations. Better by far to build up the inner fortitude of knowing that you are a one-off, beyond any comparison. And this is supportive of Truth. When you support Truth, Truth will be supportive of you. That is how true prosperity works.

DESERVING THE BEST

Another issue I come across is one of being non-deserving. Almost always, this is an inherited problem. It becomes established in a number of ways. The most common way is having grown up in a family environment of 'put downs.' Comments like, "you can't do this, you can't do that, you don't have the brains, you're not clever enough, you're not pretty enough," on and on. All this continuously repeated has a devastating effect on a child's morale. The same litany is subconsciously repeating when the child has become an adult.

If this is you, in any way at all, it is time to let go of that old pattern of conditioning. You need to overwrite the old program! You cannot have true prosperity if you hold a belief that you are non-deserving. The simple fact is, you deserve the best.

There are a lot of people who are not intellectually or academically clever. Maybe your parents told you this, over and over, and maybe it is true. So what? Wisdom comes from your heart, not your head. You do not need to be brainy to live your highest potential. I was a school dunce! You do not need academic training to know that you are a unique and beautiful Being. All that is required is correct focus, and a living application of your positive qualities.

CARE FOR YOURSELF

Another comment that comes up occasionally suggests that it is selfish to give to yourself. We should only give to other people. It is selfish to put your needs ahead of other people's needs. How this belief ever got promoted amazes me, but I expect it has a religious foundation. Tell me, how can you care for someone else if you cannot care for yourself? You have to care for yourself to even know what care is about; what it feels like to be cared for, how it nourishes you. If you are careless with yourself, holding yourself in disregard, it is not possible for you to promote caring well-being in another person. You can give them gifts, money, whatever, it matters not; true giving comes from a person's spirit, and that spiritual aspect must first be given to. This means self giving to self.

To know that you are worthy of receiving is an asset that needs developing. True giving is not about material giving - although this can be included - it is about giving from your heart. And the only heart open to truly give is the heart that is opened by receiving.

SUMMARY

You are a thinker, we all are. Fill your mind with thoughts of true prosperity. Do not mix with people who think and talk poverty. Poverty thinking is contagious. It propagates itself by lowering your morale. Think and talk always about how much is in your life. Focus on the abundance of the little things in your life, take nothing for granted. If you hold your thoughts and words toward true prosperity, this is what you are writing into your life-movie. You are a person of value and worth. Focus on this. Never talk yourself down in conversation, this is such a common error. Talk about yourself, your spouse and family, with obvious and outright pride. Elevate yourself with your true prosperity thoughts, and it will happen.

There is little that is more liberating than trust in self. It is the path to freedom from worry and anxiety, the path to true prosperity.

7 THE POWER OF TRUST

STORY TIME

Let me tell you a story about trust that I often share at my seminars. A number of years ago Treenie and I were in the U.S. traveling from Phoenix to Sedona. We were with friends, being driven in a big Silverado, when I noticed a sign on the roadside with the words; 'Slow Food.' Knowing that I detested fast food, I suggested that as it was around lunch time, we investigate the source of the sign. Following a dusty track for about a hundred meters, we arrived at a sprawling ranch-style restaurant. We entered the empty dining room, chose a table, and sat down. A very friendly waiter quickly appeared - he probably did a lot of waiting! - and took our order.

Full of enthusiasm, I walked over to the counter to tell the owners what a wonderful sight their 'Slow Food' sign was, while the waiter chatted with my friends. After spending five minutes expressing my delight at their unique, common-sense approach, I finally realised that they could not understand a word I said. They were

Hispanic, and me from Oz! Disillusioned, but unbowed, I returned to our table just as the waiter and our driver were discussing trust. How their conversation got there, I have no idea!

Subtle trust

Making eye contact with the waiter, I asked him, "Do you fully trust yourself?"

He looked embarrassed. "Er, well, no, not really. I wish I did."

I smiled. "That's okay. You have a lot of company in the world. Do you have a best friend? And if so, do you trust your best friend?"

He nodded. "I share an apartment with a guy. Right now, he's my best friend. And of course I trust him. Otherwise I wouldn't share an apartment with him."

"Very sensible. Would you trust him with your life?" I asked.

"Hmmm. That's a big one. But . . . yes, I would. He's a great guy. I trust him."

"Okay, fair enough. Would you give your life to a person whom you don't trust?"

"Well, of course not," he exclaimed. "That would be stupid. Nobody would do that!"

"Oh, yes they would," I replied. "You have. You

have given your life to yourself, and at the beginning of this conversation you told me that you do not trust yourself."

TRUSTING FRIENDS

He stared at me in astonishment. "My God, that makes me sound stupid. I . . . just didn't realise. I mean . . . wow!"

"Trust is very subtle," I told him. "I didn't set out to trap you. I wanted to reveal to you just how easy it is to think you are trusting, yet all you are doing is deceiving yourself."

He thought about it for some minutes, then asked, "What do I do about it?"

I grinned. "Now that's a good question."

We will leave the conversation at this point. My question to you is, are you like the waiter? Are you one of the majority of people who trust your best friend more than you trust yourself? A whole lot of people have a best friend simply so they can have someone in their life whom they can fully trust and depend on. This is okay - so long as you do not trust them more than you trust yourself.

I have three questions for you; would you trust a person whom you have criticised for many years? Would you trust a person whom you consider has repeatedly let you down? Would you trust a person who is incapable of making firm decisions and/or acting on them?

BEST FRIENDS!

Your answer is most probably, 'no.' Suppose that the person in question is you? On a deep level, how can you possibly trust yourself when you are always criticising yourself? Trust and criticism do not go together. Self-criticism holds hands with doubt. They are very close! Most people - to some extent - trust their best friend but doubt themselves. A lot of people go to their best friend to talk life's problems over. Fair enough, but be aware that the problems you are needing to address are 'yours,' not your friend's, and their solution may not always be in your best interest. While any other person makes your decisions for you, or seriously influences your own decisions, you are creating another dependency. This is not the way to true prosperity. Let us go back to our earlier discussion of life as energy. If you are continually seeking support from a best friend, and they continually give it to you, then even with the best of intentions, they are not offering what is best for you. Your energy field is weakened, and they are helping you to maintain its weakness.

A best friend should listen sympathetically to your

tale of woe, then, when you have finished, say, "Look, I hear what you are saying and I sympathise with your dilemma. However, it is you who needs to make the decision, not me. Whatever you decide, I'll support you. You're my best friend, and I know that you can do it." This is the friendship and support that empowers and stabilises your field of energy, strengthening it.

TRUE SUPPORT

This is the role of a best friend. This is 'real' support. If however, they literally talk you into a decision, then they are supporting your weaknesses. They are definitely 'not' your best friend! A best friend supports your strengths, helping you to gain the inner fortitude so necessary for life. And remember, you are almost certainly someone else's best friend! You need to do the same for them. When you are both *truly* best friends to each other, you walk the path of true prosperity together. If a husband and wife, or partners in a relationship can live and be like this, they grow together toward their inner strengths in a smooth unfolding. The second question was, would you trust a person who has repeatedly let you down? So, taking you as the person, it is most likely that much of your self-talk - your continuous stream of thoughts - is criticism about you continually letting yourself down.

The 'I could have done better,' or, looking back to school days, 'I wish now I had paid more attention,' or 'Damn, I blew that interview,' or 'If only I had bothered,' or, 'Gee, I'm just about hopeless' type of thoughts; all are thoughts that erode your ability to trust yourself. Add to this potent mix the conditioning from too many parents who inferred to their growing teenagers that they felt 'let down' by their sons' or daughters' lack of effort and achievement. It is all erosive.

MAJOR PLAYER

This parental criticism subconsciously continues into your adult life. You get to feel that you let them, and yourself, down. And sometimes this is a reality. Many people do betray their own best interests. However, the reinforcement of self-doubt is not the way out, it is the preparedness to trust yourself - beginning now! You *are* worthy of trust.

The third question was, would you trust a person in-capable of making, and acting on a decision? In my semi-nars I find that procrastination is a major factor in many people's lives. Perhaps this is you. A lot of people put off making a decision. If and when they do, they delay acting upon it until they are literally forced by circumstances. Again, this is the result of a lack of trust in self. This is where the best friend comes in. I repeat, a best friend gives their love and support on the decisions made, and actions taken, by you. And a best friend never says 'I told you so' if things go wrong, especially in a relationship situation. If you have a best friend like that, get them out of your life. Best friends are truly supportive.

Trust is a major player in the true prosperity game. To trust yourself, to be able to put the past behind you and move on, you need to know that it is okay, and natural to make mistakes, and simply move forward.

STAY IN THE SUNSHINE

Are you a person who believes in 'saving for a rainy day'? This is a belief that someday things will go wrong, and that you will then need money. It certainly seems to be obvious common sense, but far less obvious is the fact that this belief becomes a focus. Saving for when things go wrong is the focus and formula for creating exactly that situation. Then, of course - ignorant of your role as your life-movie creator - it gets reinforced by your saying, "Thank God I saved for just such an occasion." In reality, you create it all. It is good to save, but not for a gloomy, pessimistic, rainy day. Instead of saving for that, you can save for your special holiday, or when the opportunity to fly overseas to your relatives suddenly comes up, or for when the sunny, optimistic day arrives.

It is all about trust. Trust brings continuous sunshine into your life. Doubtful caution of things going wrong brings more gloomy days than you will ever want. Remember, you are a movie maker. If you write optimistic trust into the script, then life is supportive of your trust. If you write pessimistic expectations of something going wrong, then life will attract and support this also. Which do you want? Saving your money is sensible. Wise investment is sensible. Good financial management is sensible. I recommend all of them, but remember, the focus you create through/with your money is the focus of your personal life.

'RAINY DAY' FEAR

Another aspect of the 'rainy day' syndrome is that it promotes fear. Any action that is fear based will attract and maintain reasons for you to fear. Look at it this way - money is energy. Fear is a self-created energy. So if fear is the background cause for saving money, then you are literally creating a savings account of fear, stored and accumulated fear. This is not a good idea! This happens to people. I have often had people say to me how glad they were that they had savings for the unexpected 'accident' that had taken place in the family.

Sometimes I offer them a different view of their reality. Mostly, I do not. It depends on how open the person is. I never push Truth at people. If I feel the receptivity, I offer it. If they react with an argument, I say no more. If a person is attached to their belief, then they deserve to keep it.

I have had people tell me that they actually have an 'accident' savings, just in case it happens! I tell them that it *will* happen. They are creating the certainty of it. This is scary! What they call a common sense policy, I call an accidental certainty! A friend of mine back in the U.K. took out a life policy when he was young so that the money would be there for when he got ill. In those long ago days it seemed so sensible. Unfortunately, he needed it!

You may be thinking, does this mean if I do not save for a rainy day that I will not get one? No, it does not. What I am saying is that if you have 'rainy day' in your background focus, it is in your field of energy. This is your life. If you do not have 'rainy day' as part of your focus, it is not in your field of energy. And this is your life. Which would you prefer?

SIMPLE IS POWERFUL

Any money/energy patterns that are not supportive of you as a person, are a poor investment. Some people are afraid of having money simply because they are afraid of losing it. No matter what they do to try and accumulate money, something always seems to work against them. Unrealised, they sabotage themselves, because their fear of losing their money is greater than their fear of not having enough.

They are not so much deficient in money, as in trust! If you recognise this pattern in you, be aware that trust in yourself, trust in your abilities, and trust in life can and will end the negative focus that undermines you. You would be surprised at how common this is. We humans have become exceedingly complex and complicated in our approach to all matters pertaining to life. It does not have to be that way. Life is vast beyond all our concepts or imagination, but it is incredibly simple. Complication muddles, simple is powerful. Trust!

Imagine trust in your field of energy. Where you have the waves of disturbance that are caused by fears, doubts, greed, anger, a whole bag of negatives, all you need to do is add a large spoonful of trust. Like magic, the waves are rapidly calmed, soon to be no more than mere ripples. In many ways, it is magic! Magic which is natural to humanity. We are very inclined to scoff at magic, forgetting the magical power of our own thinking.

Essential ingredient

Trust is an essential ingredient in your true prosperity; trusting self. The lack of self-trust shows up most obviously when decisions need to be made. Being clear and decisive is not a common expression. Most people tend toward 'wait and see,' hoping life will make the decision for them. And life often does. But had you made a decision, life might have taken a very different direction, a direction which may have been more favorable.

Making decisions about your own life is very necessary. In my marriage with Treenie, we make the decisions about family, and whatever affects the two of us, together. In our personal life, we each make our own decisions, always taking the other into consideration. Even if we do not always agree with the other's decision, they are ours to make and we each respect that. We support each other, respecting and honoring our differences. We each help the other to fortify and strengthen the field of energy which manifests as the life we each live. Too many couples verbally attack or criticise each other, thus eroding and destabilising their respective fields of energy. Remember, how you treat another person has a parallel effect on your own energy field.

I have learned that it is not until you can trust yourself to make clear and definite decisions, that you can trust the decisions of your family, friends, or people close to you. When you easily make and trust your own decisions, it is equally easy to trust the decisions of another person.

IN CONTROL

Interestingly, life indicates that those people who trust their decision making always seem to make good decisions, while people who delay making decisions until under pressure do not always make such good ones. Trust in self is the vital ingredient. When trust is an integral part of your field of energy, making decisions is easy. The mind is focussed and centered in trust; trusting both self and life. (Not that there is any difference!)

Have you anyone in your life who has a need to control? Is this you? It would appear that control people have a lot of trust in themselves, and very little trust in other people. As so often happens, appearances can be deceptive. The control person holds a deep-seated fear of life. Deep in their subconscious lurks a fear of helplessness, a fear that everything is out of their control. Mostly it comes from a really nasty childhood incident, leaving such a deep impression that when the child is an adult he/she desperately attempts to control all life around him/her. This mostly means family and friends. The intent of these people is almost always beneficial, but the results are to create and maintain a degree of helplessness in the very people whom they love, and are under their controlling influence.

OUT OF CONTROL

There is a common, unsympathetic term, 'control freak.' Control people are not freaks, they are still frightened, still traumatised. Their need to control is a reaction to the unpleasant experience they endured, an experience some of them would not even remember. When a childhood trauma is really bad, emotional survival will often wipe out the conscious memory, but this does not erase the memory of the psyche. And what the psyche retains, the person's life will reflect. The impression left with them is the trauma and pain inflicted by someone 'out' of control. A compulsion to be 'in' control is a natural reaction.

If this is you, let go of the guilt. You are not to blame for what happened. It was out of 'your' control. For reasons that become too metaphysical to explore in this book, you need to accept that you wrote this into the script of your life-movie. Let us simply say that on a soul level you had an area of neglect, and you chose to strengthen it. The reaction that expresses as tight control is just that, tight and restrictive - for you. It would appear that you are limiting and restricting the people under your influence, and you are, but you are the unrealised victim. You are the person still under a control that hurt you a long time ago. And by being a controller, you remain under that old control.

FLEXIBILITY

The answer is clear and simple - let go. Simple maybe, but mostly not easy. However, reading this, and seeing a highly probable cause laid out before you, can be a prime motivator in your releasing the past. By releasing the past you are healing your now. Healing your now in turn creates a new, more relaxed and flexible future. You can do this.

Whatever happens, do not get into denial. The need to control is not a crime, it is not bad, or wrong. It is the inner child reacting to an old fear. And the inner child is powerful! You just need to accept that influencing and controlling others is not the answer. You are holding onto the problem for yourself, while creating a problem for your family and friends. And all this becomes self-perpetuating, on and on through other frames of your life-movie.

Break the pattern. Taking one day at a time, lay in bed when you wake up in the morning, and affirm that this day you will be relaxed and flexible. Today you will not make decisions and directions that are not yours to make. Today you will simply support the decisions and direction of your family and friends. Today you will - TRUST.

A STRUCTURED LIFE

Most control people set up a highly structured life for themselves and, if they can, for family and friends. Now, there is nothing wrong with structure. Nature expresses through structure and order, this is a way of life. But nature always expresses through the structure which is most appropriate for the life cycle of whatever particular form. You need flexibility in your structures. The control person generally creates a structured lifestyle that is rigid and restrictive. Looking at nature it compares with the flexibility of an oak tree. A little give and take, but a serious storm will rend and break it. And life offers us many storms!

The structure that you need is one with the flexibility of the riverside willow. When the storms rage, the willow is blown flat, bowed but unbroken. When the storm passes on, the oak's strength has been fractured, while the willow's flexibility has been reinforced.

People are inclined toward becoming specialists. The

demands of employment are inclined toward conditions where you have to learn to specialise. This is another structure. While it can be beneficial to your income, it may not be beneficial to your life and living. It may not be supportive of your marriage. It may not be beneficial to your role as a parent. In this case, your specialisation for financial purposes often has a high price tag.

What is needed is a wholistic specialisation. In nature, the creatures that become the most extreme of narrow-focussed specialists are the highest on the lists of natural extinction. I am a specialist! I specialise in the wholistic Art of Living, learning to balance and harmonise my life within the Whole.

SUMMARY

What is the structure of your life? Even if you are not a control person, is your life based in old structures that are required to endure time without any changes? Or are you flexible enough to live within a structured order that changes and responds to the needs and demands of the moment? True prosperity is about order and expression. Old and rigid ways of living mostly are a defence against life. A lack of trust. Flexibility and newness are much more inclined toward trust.

Trust is one of the greatest powers in your life; to

trust yourself. When you fully trust yourself, you are a person high in confidence. You then attract the positive people who find these qualities to be endearing. You are feeding power and certainty into your field of energy. There is little that is more liberating than trust in self. It is the path to freedom from worry and anxiety, the path to true prosperity. You cannot trust and be anxious. If you are anxious, you are not trusting; if you are trusting, then anxiety is a stranger. If you want to measure your ability to trust, that is the scale you use. You cannot anxiously trust!

Realise that life is supportive of you. Life is not a cosmic accident; life is a design of intelligence. Trust in self is an expression of that same intelligence.

N o matter how bad it
may seem, or how
overwhelming life may appear,
nothing will ever happen to you
that is not for your ultimate
benefit.

8 FEAR: A SELF-DEFEATING FOCUS

Negative weapons

There is nothing more debilitating and humiliating in our lives than our various fears. It is obvious that fear and true prosperity have nothing in common. Fear is probably the single most common factor in humanity. We have all experienced it, and most people will live with it every day of their lives. So what is fear? I go back to the American I quoted earlier in these pages: FEAR - False Evidence Appearing Real. This is as close and accurate as you are ever going to get. Fear is not reality-based, it is the power of illusions, falsity.

Let us return to our overall theme: you are the asset in your life, not money. Money is the result of good self-management. The very worst expression that can be introduced into your self-management is fear. Fear is frequently used as a weapon. U.S. presidents use it, telling the press of all the fearful things that could happen to the economy and lifestyle if we do not do this or that. Governments and their political opposition use it, attempting to win elections by creating a monster of fearful expectations if they are not elected. The media likes nothing better than fear news to trumpet to the nations. Fear is a negative-based energy, always begetting more to be fearful about.

HUMILIATION

I, like most people, had a long list of fears. Some were simply the leftovers from my youth, and were soon resolved, others were more persistent. I had a deep and abiding fear of being inadequate. At a seminar, or Retreat, I sometimes jokingly say that we are each given a certain quota of fears, and that I faced my fears so constantly and repeatedly that by the time I was forty-nine they were all used up. Let me clearly affirm that all fears are our own creation. Most human energy fields are saturated in fear, and all based in falsity.

Your fears have to be faced, and challenged. Some are just old habits, not even valid! Let me share another personal story about facing one of my fears. I have mentioned my fear of matriarchal women, and how I dealt with that. That was quick and, as it happened, easy. This one was neither quick nor easy, taking place around the mid 1980's.

One day Treenie and I were in our nearby coastal

town and, having finished our shopping, we were about to return home. As we drove through the town, we passed the local unemployment centre, and I noticed a queue of people reaching outside onto the pavement. In Oz we call unemployment benefits the 'dole.' This is what the queue was for. As we drove past I looked at the people with contempt, and for the first time realized just how much I would hate and fear publicly queuing for the dole. For me, then, it would be the ultimate humiliation. But as we drove past, I had to face the fact that in reality, I was on the dole! I was without money, and unemployed. I received the biweekly government handout.

NOT JUSTIFIED

The people in the queue were local. I lived far enough away that I was one of those allowed to receive the dole by mail, instead of having to physically be at the unemployment centre. As I realised the breadth and depth of my fear, I had to face my hypocrisy. How could I regard them with contempt? I was no better than the people in the queue. The reality shocked me so much that I resolved that from then on I would go to the benefits centre and stand in the dole queue. In this way I would face my fear.

Later, attempting to trace where this contempt came

from, I had to journey back into the days of my youth. My father was a very complex man. One part of him would be helping the down and out, generously giving money to them, while at the same time another part of him held them in contempt. I am sure, today, that he did not mean to be contemptuous. I have no doubt that it came from his ingrained puritanical work ethic. However, I heard his remarks enough times to impress into me his contempt for the unemployed. "There's always work if you're prepared to look for it, or do anything," he would say. And I am sure he was right, but this does not justify contempt. Unknown and unrealized, I picked up, and carried, a contempt for the unemployed, along with its accompanying blame and fear. Finally, all those years later my soul growth demanded that it must be faced and dealt with.

UNEMPLOYMENT

Treacherously nestled within my contempt for others, was my own fear of being regarded with contempt. In the 1980's the people of Oz were rather unforgiving of people on the dole. They called them 'dole bludgers.' A colloquial expression, meaning someone who would rather take a handout than work for a living. Today that attitude has basically changed, there is now far more sympathy and tolerance toward the unemployed.

I will never forget the first time I went and joined the dole queue. As it happened, the queue was long, and I had to join it in the doorway. I stood and cringed, terrified that someone would walk or drive past who would recognise me. It never even occurred to me that they might not care. When you have a fear, your reality is literally built on the foundations of that fear. I noticed that the men in my age group, around the mid-forties, just stared at the ground, slowly moving forward in what seemed a shuffle of shame. Like me, most of those men were deeply humiliated by the whole sorry process.

The weeks passed so fast that I constantly seemed to be in the biweekly dole session. For a long time I cringed in that queue, feeling shame, anger, hurt, and blame. I blamed myself. I was proving to the world that I was inadequate, a failure, reduced to being nothing more than a dole bludger. I really laid it on, thick and fast.

Gradually however, I began to reassess myself. Blame did not help, nor did smashing what little self-esteem still survived. I began to accept that this was an unwanted inheritance, and there was no blame attached. Not to anyone.

A DIFFERENT OUTLOOK

I began to look on this as a challenge. After all, I chose to face my fear to resolve it, not to further reduce myself by massive self-criticism. I made a deliberate effort to stand straight and tall in the dole queue. Instead of avoiding the eyes of others, I made eye contact and smiled encouragingly. I noticed that teenagers who had just left school were not in the least bit concerned by being on the dole, they had a totally different outlook on life. This is not to say that their outlook was better, they had their own issues to deal with, but they did not carry the guilt and shame synonymous to men of my age when out of work and money. I changed my outlook. I accepted that this was a passing phase in my life, and that this too would pass. I decided not to berate and flog myself, but to treat myself kindly.

The results were fast and positive. It took me eighteen months of standing in that queue twice a month, and I no longer had the problem. What I did not expect was the gift that life gave me, in appreciation of my efforts. I learned compassion. In my life I had often acted compassionately to others, but it was always an act. Now I could *be* compassionate.

A NEGATIVE REACTION

Experience has shown me that any fear which is faced is proved to be an impostor. I suspect that one of the greatest fears for most people is a fear of the unknown. The unknown is Mystery, seemingly filled with threat and fright. I am not saying that the unknown is frightening - it is not - but that is the common reaction. Remember, fear is always a negative reaction. You react to the unknown. There are people who embrace the unknown, seeking thrills in risky travels and thrill adventures, but they also have their own different fears to contend with.

Let us now look at fear in relationship to money. All too often they go hand in hand. Fear of not having enough money. Fear of not being able to earn enough money. Fear of having so much money you may lose some. Fear that you did not inherit the talent to keep the money you inherited. Fear that friends are attracted by your money, not you. Fear of taxation. Fear that . . . the list is long and complicated. It is unfortunate that with so many fears it is all too easy for fear to become a prime focus in your life. Fear is menacing and debilitating. It can reduce you to human wreckage. Fear takes a tremendous amount of energy from your energy field, weakening and destroying you and your life. Yet despite that, to a lesser or greater degree, fear is the motivator in most people's lives. When the negative potential of fear is introduced into the financial aspect of a person's life, the result can be financial and/or personal chaos.

FINANCIAL FEARS

As much as you can, be aware of the fear element in your financial affairs. Try to calculate to what extent you are fear motivated, or fear driven. If you can truly say that these do not apply in your life, you are indeed fortunate. You are also well along the path toward true prosperity. I had to face and deal with fear as the motivator when I was milking cows, plus my fear of the unknown when I was traveling around Oz. Heaps and lashings of the unknown every day. That was another part of my insecurity. Dear old Dad! "Security, my son, is money . . ." The unknown always seemed to hold negatives in those days - that was my outlook. For me, the unknown meant financial ruin. The idea that the unknown could offer me wonderful prospects was scarcely even a dream.

In general, the value of your self-worth equals the measure of your financial income. If you have low self-worth almost certainly your income will be low. But people are very complex. You may be a person on a high income, basing your self-worth on your financial worth. This is quite common, a massive form of self-deceit. If this is you, you only have to lose that high income, and your self-worth plummets also. The name of the game is to have high self-worth/esteem, which in turn will generate an income high enough for your lifestyle.

HUMAN VALUES

I am very familiar with the 'a person is worth the money they earn' syndrome. My father always used to scan the weekend column of obituaries in the newspaper. In those days they reported the age of the person at death, along with their financial status. Dad used to read out the more well-known ones, especially any local farmers from our local newspaper. I can hear him now, as he read them to my mother: "Fancy that, James Williams has died. You remember Jim, don't you darling. He was only fifty-five. I always said he didn't look a healthy man. He left three hundred thousand pounds. Hmmmm, he did well! He was more successful than I thought." And so it would continue down the obituary column. All too soon, at sixty-three he took his turn in that column. I wonder what comments were made about him, age and value.

I had to find my self-worth while my income was low to zero. This is a tough way to do it. Again, I recommend that you reassess your worth, realising that your value as a person in no way equates to money earned, owned, gained, or lost. A good, strong sense of self-worth throws a positively attractive quality into your field of energy. This, in turn, attracts energies toward you that will maintain and even improve the quality of your life. These energies may translate as opportunities for work improvement, a raised salary, beneficial investments, etc. Basically, life will meet you where you are 'at,' improving your life in a way that relates to you, your family, or your lifestyle.

Two common illusions

When I share some of my story at a True Prosperity seminar, many people are surprised that I can be so open about my so-called, 'down' times, times that society would quickly label as failure. I do not see life in terms of success or failure. I see life in terms of overall experience. Judging a person according to their financial status is a ridiculous way to evaluate a person's life. It must reign almost supreme as a measure of ignorance. For as long as you measure life in terms of success or failure, you remain unenlightened.

During our years of so-called financial poverty, I had no choice but to face my heap of financial fears. I had to face my low self-esteem, and my fear of failure. In those days I believed in failure, and all its illusions. I remember one day during our four years when we lived in an intentional community, I was sitting alone on my bed having an anxiety attack. Our financial situation was at rock bottom, and I was in an emotional and mental stew, with the heat turned up! Although we owned a small piece of steep, seemingly unsellable land in Tasmania, our bank account was down to about $200. This was early in December, and with four children, I was trying to work out how we could financially manage Christmas.

BETTER OR WORSE!

So there I sat, contemplating a bleak Christmas in a complete funk, when Treenie walked into our room. She looked very serious. "Do you have any idea how much we have in our bank account?" she asked, in what sounded like accusatory tones.

Although I thought I knew, I replied, "No, how much?"

Her expression even more serious, she said, "$4," and walked out of the room.

I felt as though I had been hit by a car, the shock was so great. For long moments I could not grasp the reality of what she said. When I did I was truly overwhelmed. My previous anxiety attack had been a mere trial run! The stew pot heat had suddenly been turned to superhigh. The surge of fear, the overwhelming shock, the shame and humiliation, was so sudden and massive that I lost consciousness. I did not faint, I just passed out. That did not help one little bit. When I came to, the situation remained unchanged!

When I write a book, I am not a head and theory person. I have been there. My heart, my concern, and my experience is in my words when I reaffirm: no matter how bad it may seem, or how overwhelming life may appear, nothing will ever happen to you that is not for your ultimate benefit. This may seem odd. It may seem impossible, but let me assure you that the cake we call life is multilayered, and every flavour is added for a reason. The cake is the sum of its many ingredients, and when sufficient heat is applied to those odd, seemingly unlikely ingredients, alchemy is invoked. What comes from the heat of experience is far more than the sum of the initial ingredients. This is life!

ABOUT SERVICE

As difficult as it may be, do not judge yourself in any way that is related to your financial income. In fact, do not judge yourself - or anyone else - for any reason at all. It all leads to grief, fear, and more illusions.

In seminars I meet quite a lot of dedicated people

who judge their worth by the service they perform for other people. In further conversation they sometimes indicate that they have a low income. I have heard this said with a sense of pride! Their income relates to the value of their worth, according to the service they give. Very rarely do I find that these people feel that they have given enough. They have an 'Of course, I could do more' attitude. In other words, a subtle way of saying, 'I'm not yet good enough from giving.' Be clear, I am not saying this applies to all people involved in service work or charitable institutions. Not at all. There are many saints out there, giving from open hearts filled with love and care.

However, life does not give financial reward for goodness, or acts of charity. It simply does not work that way. Ask any wealthy corporate crook, or legal embezzler! I have spoken to service people who are sorely puzzled that their income has not risen as a result of their charity. My father was a charitable man, but it made not a mote of difference to his income. The pathway from the large entrance gates up to the main door at Trumpington Church used to be deep, loose gravel, and it was extremely difficult to push a wheelchair along it. My father paid a considerable sum for the pathway to be sealed with bitumen, making the access far easier. He told me himself that the following year was one of the worst harvests he ever had. I remember, very indignantly, saying, "You would think that God would know better!"

A KICK IN THE HEART

People come into conflict with financial flow very easily. It seems that there is a multitude of reasons both why and how we turn off the tap of financial abundance. Children have far less of a problem with this than adults. They see life more simply, more clearly.

My granddaughter, Jacinta, was about six years of age when she began busking for money. Actually, her mother sat in a cafe while Jacinta played her violin outside. Because it attracted customers, the cafe owners liked the arrangement. Cute as only a little girl can be, she played her instrument with verve and skill, not in the least embarrassed or shy. On average, she made about a dollar a minute in a small country town! Her smile is a kick in the heart, and people loved her. One day, when she was talking to Jaspher, her brother who is a couple of years older, she was overheard to say, "Isn't it wonderful, Jaspher, the way that life just throws money at you." Her usual playing time was around thirty minutes, and with the money she earned she has bought herself a bicycle, some clothes, and she paid for another girl to go on a whale watching outing. She has it all together! At this stage in her life, money is a heart affair. I only hope it stays that way.

A HIGHER POWER

One aspect of the service to others that I have come across is 'giving to a higher power.' Basically, this means giving to God. One man proudly told me that he gave much of his income to God, but he could not understand why he continued to financially struggle. I asked him, rather bluntly, if he expected to buy heavenly favours. He was very indignant - and he looked very guilty! Seriously, you cannot do this. All he was doing was trying to buy his way out of financial fear. Fear uses every disguise in the book.

Another woman told me she was happy to give to God and charity, but she had real trouble in giving to herself. I asked her if she felt worthy. After a lot of tears, the answer was no. And again, it all began in her childhood. In her household, God was everything, people were nothing. Such vast ignorance amazes me. She could not give to herself because she was terrified by her indoctrinated, 'demands of God.' She asked me where she fit into all this.

I suggested that if this God of hers was a God of love - which she affirmed - then God would get immense pleasure if she gave to herself. I justified it for her by telling her that obviously God loves her, for love is the pure nature of God. Unable to find a loophole, she was overwhelmed with joy, crying tears of sheer relief and release. A year later, after thanking me profusely, she told me that her whole life was wonderfully uplifted and changed.

If you have been inadvertently taught to fear, you must acknowledge this, and move away from it. Giving to yourself financially has its own need and importance. You have as much right and need to receive financial abundance as you do to receive spiritual abundance. There is no conflict of interest here unless you are fear motivated. Fear takes from; it withdraws from your abundance account. Live from your heart, give from your heart - both to yourself and others - and you are in the spiritual flow of true prosperity.

SUMMARY

Remember those previously mentioned words; FEAR - False Evidence Appearing Real. Whenever fear starts your stomach churning, remember that it is *always* based in falsity, not in Truth. I am so full of admiration for the truth of those four words, that I would like to offer a few more. False Evidence Appearing Real identifies the nature of the problem, my offering suggests how you can deal with it; FEAR - Face it, Evaluate, Act, Relax.

My meaning is this: Face the fear, admit the fear, and Evaluate how you can best Act from a heart/love/trust expression. When you have determined this, Act on it immediately, do not procrastinate. Then Relax. Simply let go. Trust yourself, your decision, and your actions.

You can never beat fear. There are no techniques to overcome it. You can neither run from it, deny it, nor banish it. Why? Because fear is your own creation. While you in any way oppose fear, you affirm, feed and nourish it. What you can do - eventually - is choose not to create fear. In knowing the Truth of Self and life, fear is no longer relevant. Fear lives in, and is, illusion. Never let fear be the reason for your daily actions. Trust yourself, use your courage, face whatever it is that seems so threatening, and dare to live a life that honours you.

*I*t has been my experience that if you follow your heart expression, life is very supportive, whereas following other people's expectations of you inevitably leads you to disappointment.

9   TO YOUR SELF, BE TRUE

FROM THE PAST

One of the more difficult things that you face in your adult life is - as I have often mentioned - putting aside all the negative beliefs, expectations, approval, conditioning, fears, dogma, and attitudes of your parents. Only the negative, because on the positive side your parents have or had many wonderful qualities to pass on. It sounds reasonably simple, but of course, most people do just the opposite.

The best, most positive qualities are so easily dismissed, taken for granted, part of a pattern that is somehow overlooked. But the negative aspects! Wow! Every family reunion has a little group discussing the parental idiosyncrasies and faults. Nobody in these gossip groups ever seems to realise that the more they focus on the negative issues of their parents, the more these aspects show up in themselves. In fact, the issues that most bother you in your parents, or a parent, are the aspects that you most dislike in yourself, and your life.

After listening to many stories of parental abuse, in the following discussion I always reach the point where I say, "Look, this is all in the past. You can blame forever, and be justifiably correct, but right now you have a life to live and get on with."

A PROMISE

While you live your life blaming a parent, you are not *living* your life. You are throwing away life's precious moments. You are throwing away opportunities to move on, to develop the potential that is within you. You are becoming that parent you most focus on, along with all their negative issues. The person whom you could be is reduced by resentment and blame.

Believe me, I have heard some horror stories about people's fathers, bad enough to really shock me, but even this does not take away from a basic reality; what we most dwell on in our memories and emotions becomes the focus of our lives. And what we focus on, we attract. So many people focus on, and are angry about their father's alcoholism, never once realising that they are an alcoholic in the making. Anger, blame, and resentment love the taste and tumult of alcohol. Unwittingly, you set the whole scene up to again be repeated.

My father - here I go again, my father! To allay any

misunderstanding, my father was a man that to this day I love, respect, and admire. His father died when he was two, his mother never remarried, so he had no idea what a father role consisted of when his children were born. What I admire is that he did his best as a father, and more you cannot do.

So, my father had a quick temper, and when he was sufficiently angry with me, he would use a cane, or his leather belt to beat me. On the odd, rare occasion, he did not know when to stop. The hurt and outrage of it impressed into me. When I became a father, remembering this, I made myself a promise that I would never beat/punish any of my children in anger. I kept my promise. In this way, I was true to myself, not to a negative aspect of my father. His negative aspects that I picked up have been deliberately released, yet to this day I see many of his positive qualities in me, and I delight in them.

TOO YOUNG TO KNOW

At seminars, men in their thirties often approach me to discuss their working life. Most of them specialise in whatever it is they do, but their issue is, they hate it. It seems quite a common problem. In our western systems of education, teenagers at high school are expected to choose the professional career they will work at for the rest of their lives, and then do preliminary study for it. Some know exactly what they want to do, they have grown up knowing. But more often than not the choice is made by looking at what is most available on the job market. Many influences determine this; parental bias, father's or mother's career, work security, glamor, compatible skills, someone admired, whatever guarantees the highest possible rate of financial income, plus your current self-worth and self-esteem.

What a crass and inadequate criteria to determine the whole of your working life. This is the time that will have the greatest influence on your true prosperity. And to make matters even worse, in the mid-to-late teens you have no idea what life is about! No idea of your wider possibilities or deepest potential. All you have is hopes, concepts - and fears. Sure, there is also excitement, but the trepidation is greater. Comparatively few will follow the quiet dictates of their heart, their inner creativity.

The choice is made, the student goes to university, and the qualifications are earned. For a few years all goes well, then tedium, boredom, and the scary thought, "Is this what I'm supposed to do for the rest of my life?" Some find it easy, at any age, to change their profession, others feel that they should stick with it, while some are plain scared to change. One man told me that he detested what he was doing, asking me what he should do about it. I knew he was in his late thirties.

"Quit," I suggested. "What would you like to do?"

"I can't quit," he said. "My parents will throw a fit. They tell me repeatedly that they spent thousands on my education, and that they are proud of me."

"So you need their approval, plus you accept the guilt they shovel at you?" I asked.

He looked miserable. "I'll be letting them down."

"But it's okay to let yourself down?" I put to him.

He shrugged. "I'm stuck."

I looked him in the eyes. "You have to decide whose life you are going to live, yours or your parents. I repeat, what would you like to do?"

He had no idea. That is how out-of-touch with himself he was. After quite a long talk, while I bolstered his courage and pepped up his vision, I told him to be true to himself. This way he would put his best into life, and get the best back in return.

EXPECTATIONS

I find it very sad when a man or woman in their thirties or forties are living a life that is a complete lie to them. True prosperity requires that you live true to yourself. If you are married, almost certainly there are compromises to be made, but they should not be about your chosen career, your life path, especially if you enjoy it. And your profession is very much part of your life path. Do not get stuck with needing parental approval (which is mostly father based) by going against your own creative desires. Follow your heart, be true to yourself. It has been my experience that if you follow your heart expression, life is very supportive, whereas following other people's expectations of you inevitably leads you to disappointment. Life does not support you living against yourself. It cannot, because by doing so you are sowing discord and conflict into your field of energy.

Some people have strange expectations. I have met people who have decided that they can be spiritual or materialistic, but they cannot have, or be, both. How crazy is that? To be sure, if that is what you believe, you will be right, because you are the director of your life-movie. You will make it so. But it does not have to be that way. I am a deeply spiritual man, and financially sound; both are balanced within my true prosperity. Each is a need that we all have. Making a choice between one or the other is creating limitation and denial in your life. Open yourself to life in a more wholistic way, meeting all your needs abundantly. Once life receives a new, more open focus from you, the flow of abundance will begin.

WORKING MODE

To live a spiritually focussed life within the work force is not difficult, but it does mean that you have to be true to self, rather than just being income focussed. I have met men with no income focus at all, men who considered themselves stuck in a working mode, simply earning whatever pay packet they can get. Generally, they very much underrate themselves. Self-worth and self-esteem are often an issue. If being a manual worker is not what you want, then decide what you would like to do, and go to evening classes and study. Get the necessary qualifications. Or, decide what small business you would like to be in, then save to either start, or buy it. Make sure you study and learn about financially running a small business. Far too many people overlook the need to become proficient and comfortable with every aspect of financial management. Seriously, this is what ninety-five percent of any small business is about; the management of money and time. Create and maintain a constant positive focus, knowing that anything you set your heart on, you can achieve. Remember, this is *your* life, *you* get to choose. Instead of grumbling about life, exercise your right to choose and change it. Be prepared to work toward whatever you want in life.

Some men are drifters, and it suits them. This is okay. There are no rights or wrongs in any of this, simply the actions and the consequences. As I have said, true prosperity is not about getting the greatest possible income. You can be a manual worker on a lower income, and you can experience true prosperity. It is the *quality* of your life that is the criteria to live a wholistic life based on love and integrity. By expressing these finer qualities as your foundation, abundance flows into your life in ways that will constantly surprise you. Needs are met in the most unexpected, and unlikely manner. This is the magic and mystery of living true to your deeper, most loving, self.

SUPPORT OR SABOTAGE

I have had people tell me that they cannot improve themselves financially, basically because they lack the intellectual capacity for study. Often, this is a cop-out, a put-down. It mostly comes from your childhood, from parents who have repeatedly said that you are not clever enough. You believed it, and go on to prove them right! If this is you, then you have to begin to live in a way that is self-supportive, not self-sabotaging. You need to focus on your abilities, and know that if you have a realistic ambition that is meaningful to you, then you can definitely achieve it. And I do mean realistic. It is pointless to set an unreachable goal; this is classic self-sabotage. Focus on achievable goals, and trust in yourself. Remember, anxiety is about a lack of trust in self. I have had people say that although they trust themselves, they do not trust life. This is nonsense! When you trust self, you will find that you trust life. Self and life are not separate, they are One.

However, there are the men and women who are definitely not intellectually clever enough to own their own business, or to achieve a high income position in the workforce. But this is not a negative situation. Genuinely not clever enough to be a high income achiever is in no way a handicap to achieving a lifestyle of true prosperity. Everything which is of the greatest human value is available to you. The ability to love - your self-respect and self-worth - your emotional stability - the ability to care for other people - the ability to be a person of integrity, admired by all who know you - the ability to be a wonderful parent and spouse, or partner - the ability to be a supremely worthwhile human Being - the ability of commitment - the ability to express a full and loving heart - the list is very long, and none of them require money. Money can buy none of these. Money can, in fact, get in the way, and it frequently does. Focus on what is achievable for you, and go for it.

CLARITY

One of the inner abilities that is very important for true prosperity, is clarity. To be clear in both your thinking, and your actions. So many people seem to live in a mental haze, with no clarity about anything they do, or would like to do. Generally, the one thing they are clear about is what they do not like. The reverse would be okay! To be clear about what you do like, and want, is a good focus, but clarity about what you do not like is a destructive focus. It is time for some more honest self-appraisal. Are you clear about you, your life, and what you would like to achieve? Because if you are not, be sure that it will not happen.

If you were somewhere in the centre of Oz, and you wanted to get to Sydney, the capitol city of New South Wales, but you did not know any of those details, or how to get there, how would you go about it? Would you try to hitch a ride, 'to a big city that is somewhere or other a long way from here?' Obviously, with such a lack of clarity, it could be a very long journey! Not a bad journey, or a wrong journey, but it would take a long while.

As it is with your journey as a person in life, so it is with your journey as a soul. As a person, you need to be clear about what you want out of life, what you can give to life, and how best to achieve this. Clarity! As a soul, you have clarity. Your soul purpose is to grow into the realisation of Self, learning the laws of manifestation, and to experience the Oneness of all life. Maybe you are aware of this, maybe not. If you are aware, then you know that love and trust in Self creates a clear, fulfilling, and meaningful path. If you are not aware of your soul purpose, simply focussing on creating wealth, almost certainly you will come into conflict with your own inner essence, your soul purpose.

RAGS TO RICHES

There used to be a saying in England that I remember from a boy: From rags to riches and back in three generations. I have not heard that in a long time. Not to be taken too literally, it nevertheless has a solid foundation behind it. I remember my father talking about families that had experienced this. And I have seen it since. It goes something like this: A man, comparatively uneducated, and from a working background, has the special flair to be a financial wizard. He has the 'Midas' touch, everything he invests in turns to gold. He becomes exceedingly wealthy, building a huge business and corporate empire, until he finally retires into old age, leaving the business empire to his son. The son has had the benefit of the very best education, is well-grounded and trained in business management, and he takes over the reins. He, however, lacks that outstanding "Midas' touch. He is skilled and controlled, but he is no business tycoon. Anxiety builds in him as he sees the business empire slowly stagnating. His bold bids for growth seem either in bad timing, or simply bad luck, but their fortunes slump. At fifty-five he has a massive heart attack, and in turn, his son takes over.

RICHES TO RAGS

This son has not particularly wanted to inherit the corporate empire. He too, has had the best education, yet he struggled to get through university. His heart is in the open country, and city corporate life is not what he wants. But, he is taught and trained to follow his inheritance. Slowly, very slowly, the next decade sees the corporate giant gradually fold in on itself, one part after the other sold off to maintain the essential foundation from which it was all built. The third generation son learns that his grandfather was a self-made man, and that his roots were in the countryside, in farming. He visits the ancestral home of his family, learning of simple country relatives that he did not know existed. Somehow, his line of the family had made a clean break from their family roots, almost as though in shame.

The son returns to the city and sells his remaining

shares and ownership to a keen and interested tycoon, and the family name of corporate wealth and power is released, sliding into obscurity. The son returns to the country, his needs amply met and fulfilled as a farmer.

What the story highlights is that although you can inherit wealth, either moderate or great, you may not inherit the particular set of genes that created it. And without them, it is often lost. In many ways, the grandfather was a fulfilled man, hopefully following his joy as he created the business empire, while the father struggled to do what was expected of him. The stress and anxiety destroyed his health. The grandson followed his inheritance of wealth for a while, then decided that he did not have the required skills, nor did he want them. He followed his heart back to the land. Like his grandfather, he too was a 'successful' man.

TRAPPINGS OF SUCCESS

The grandfather was true to himself, so was the grandson, while the father of the generation in between failed to acknowledge that he did not have the essential flair. Just possibly, you may see yourself somewhere in this story. I have written it in such a way that the moral is glaringly obvious; to your own self, be true. Without a doubt you will have heard of another little saying that comes in here, so common it has become a cliché; the trappings of success! What the grandfather created became a trap for his son, and he remained trapped by his father's success. Yet, although the grandson inherited his position in the trap, he was able to escape, simply by being true to self.

Simple maybe, over simple you may think, but a word of caution; the greatest truths are the simplest. So glaringly simple that human cleverness misses it altogether. Remember, simple holds hands with wisdom, clever holds hands with stupid!

SAVINGS AND ATTACHMENTS

Strange as it may seem, some people are almost obsessed by what they can leave for their children. They scrimp and save their money, spending little on themselves, and putting it aside for the children to eventually inherit. This baffles me. Why? I have nothing against your children inheriting any wealth and property you may leave them, but I certainly recommend that you live your life in a way that meets all your needs. The obsessive idea of leaving the greatest amount of money possible for the children suggests that the father, or mother, has a deep fear that their children are inadequate. This, in turn, suggests that the fear of inadequacy is based in, and about, themselves. Obsessive saving for the children, while denying yourself, could be the very worst thing that ever happened for them. Another saying puts it nicely; easy come, easy go! You value what you earn and struggle for. Not only are you denying yourself true prosperity, but you are probably also making it impossible for your children. Let your inheritance to them be one of love, and a strong sense of self-worth.

Attachments are common to people. We easily become attached to 'things,' people, ideas, beliefs, places, etc. Some people have an attachment to outcomes. If you are going into business, or choosing a new job, what is your basis of choice? Are you going to enjoy the day-to-day work, gaining job satisfaction, or are you looking ahead to 'what may be' with an ever growing attachment to an eventual outcome. You may, for example, take a job working at something that you dislike, but you are sure that promotion will come quickly and change everything. That is an attachment that will invariably lead to disappointment. It will not lead you anywhere that is even in the vicinity of true prosperity.

Take a job that you enjoy doing - in the day-to-day moment. Where it leads does not matter, but joy and fulfilment in the moment is the place of magic. An attachment to a future expectation, or hope, is a way to disaster.

FOLLOW YOUR POTENTIAL

Of all the people I read about in the work force, one of the groups that consistently comes across as people fulfilled, are those who sell real estate. I guess you can only sell if you enjoy what you are doing, and that enjoyment is the key to sales. It rubs off on the client. Mostly, they are people happy in what they are doing, and true to themselves.

This is the key to true prosperity. If you are working at some job you dislike, 'just waiting until things get better,' or for whatever other reason, get out of it, now. Be true to you. You are unique. You are worthwhile. Do not set a pattern for the frames of your life-movie that is based in 'waiting,' or 'putting off,' or 'undervaluing yourself,' or assuming that you 'don't have the brains.' If you do not like your image, change it to an image that you do like. Just remember, however, you are not an image.

SUMMARY

To be true to yourself you must be truly honest with yourself. If you are aware of certain limitations in your character - not flaws - just limits, then work within the parameters that you are comfortable with. But do not be afraid to constantly push at your own boundaries. The more efficient you become in your comfort zone, the more likely it is that you will exceed the parameters of your belief. Be prepared to stretch into the discomfort zone, and see how you handle it. This does not mean doing work that is really distasteful to you, or disliked, but taking yourself into areas that you can enjoy, but are very challenging. It will not be too long before you find that your ability exceeds your expected limitations. This is a way of real growth. Does the seed have prior knowledge of its full potential, or does it simply grow into its power? Try it, and find out!

*T*he big majority of wealthy
people are focussed on the
acquisition and growth of their
wealth assets. It is the very
few who embrace a wholistic
lifestyle within their wealth
focus.

10 SPENDING HEALTH FOR WEALTH

THE COST OF HEALTH

Statistics indicate that of the three trillion dollars spent on health care in the U.S. each year, eighty percent is spent during the last thirty days of the patient's life. To me, this is astonishing. This vast amount of money is uselessly spent on medicinal drugs, when palliative care should be the focus and priority. How ironic that the process of death has given birth to what is probably the world's biggest drug industry.

The money mentioned is allegedly spent on 'health care.' Nonsense! It is spent on sickness management, and there is a huge difference. How can you care for health if you have lost it? I have read research that claims there are ten thousand known diseases in humanity, while another figure quoted by similar research is closer to forty thousand. Ten, forty, or however many thousands in between, it indicates that we are nations of sick people. Out of curiosity, I have asked a few qualified veterinary surgeons if they have any idea of the number of diseases in animals in general. They tell me that in their studies and experience, maybe around fifty to one hundred.

Let us double that and say two hundred diseases for animals. And being conservative, around twenty thousand for us humans. What is going on? Are we crazy, or what? The vast majority of people are completely uninterested in their own health and well-being. Why? The sheer neglect of the average person for their own emotional, mental, and physical health indicates that our overall value of self is close to zero. Think about it. In Oz, statistics show that over three-quarters of a million people are on anti-depressants. I have no figures for the U.S., but it would be many millions. Zero self-worth, with its accompanying sicknesses and depression, are inseparable.

Depressed people commit suicide. In Oz, more people commit suicide than are killed in road collisions. Obvious as it may seem, we do not thrive on neglect, yet we live with shocking neglect for ourselves. In Oz, the number one killer for the past sixty years is heart disease. This says a lot. The neglected heart. Cancer, of course, is high on the list, but the heart never gets cancer. And it is the heart that I want to focus on.

HEARTS AIN'T JUST HEARTS!

According to The American Medical Association Journal, in the U.S. someone dies every thirty-two seconds from heart disease. Apparently sixty million people have it, which means about one in three. Self-neglect! Today, a coronary by-pass is common, at a cost in the region of US$30,000. It is such an everyday occurrance that talking about a relative's heart by-pass, or a President's heart by-pass, are of merely 'passing' (pardon the pun!) interest. But how many realise just what the words 'heart by-pass' are really saying? Consider also the common term, 'heart attack.' This implies that the heart suddenly, without warning, attacks its owner. I do not think so! To be more aware, we should call it 'terminal heart neglect.'

We live in strange times. Human sickness is regarded as normal, while perfect health is something you are 'lucky' to have. Extraordinary! Neglect is dismissed, luck is elevated. The way I see it, luck is the meeting place of preparation and opportunity. You make your own luck, just as you either live with good health as a focus and priority, or you neglect it. Guess which most people do? How about you? In the early 1970's, an American doctor suffered a series of myocardial arrests (heart attacks). As a result, he changed his life and, it must be added, the lives of many other people. His name was Dr. Joe

Nichols. One of his favourite comments was, "You can eat what you like for the first forty years of your life, but you pay the price with the next forty years." These days, I would say that after the first forty years of self-neglect you have few years left. Self-neglect equates with heart attack. The price is very high; shocking pain followed by death, or, prolonged suffering, operations, and a severely reduced quality of life.

A PASSED-BY HEART

A heart by-pass is exactly that; an indication that we have lived in such a way that we have by-passed all thought, care, and respect for our soul-self. Neglect! Modern heart research is indicating that the heart is the seat of the soul; that the heart is the seat of intelligence; that the heart can receive and transmit communication from one person to another; that the heart communicates with every cell in the body . . . there is far more. The heart is much more than just a biological pump, it is at the very essence of our Being. Metaphysicians have known this for thousands of years, welcoming this 'new' breakthrough heart research that resides precariously on the razor edge of medical acceptance.

DANGER ZONE

Remember the comment by Dr. Joe Nichols? Statistics show that once people hit forty, they enter the zone of the seven major diseases which lead to the death of more than eighty percent of the population; heart disease, cancer, stroke, diabetes, arthritis, osteoporosis, and Alzheimer's disease. It is estimated that someone is dying of cancer every three seconds. We talk of hardening of the arteries causing heart attacks, yet when the arteries serving the brain gradually harden, denying an adequate flow of blood to the brain, we call the resulting seizure a stroke. Surely this is a brain attack! However, enough is enough. Rather than give you statistical 'constipation' - chronic constipation is probably the fundamental cause of most disease - a final one makes my point; eighty percent of those seven major diseases, plus the many thousands of other diseases, are caused by ingesting inappropriate food/drink choices. You can add smoking. More neglect! In other words, we create our own diseases, our own pain and suffering, by sheer self-neglect!

The big majority of wealthy people are focussed on the acquisition and growth of their wealth assets. It is the very few who embrace a wholistic lifestyle within their wealth focus. It could be truly said that the majority spend their health to gain their wealth. This is a very poor trade. True prosperity is about health first, wealth has its place as a secondary need. I do not mean wealth as sufficient financial income, I mean wealth as defined in a dictionary; "a great amount of accumulated money." How much wiser it would be to have a great amount of accumulated health!

HUNTER/GATHERER

In many people there is a real hunger for wealth. This unrecognised hunger has many ways of expressing, and whilst a drive for wealth is the most apparent, an emotional hunger is also generated. This subtle form of hunger craves high fat and high sugar foods. Unrealised, this hunger kicks in an old, deeply buried, subconscious program of survival. And survival instincts crave fat and sugar. For the early hunter/gatherers, this equated with natural foods, such as animal fat and pure honey. Not so the modern hunter/gatherer. His or her hunting ground is the world of corporate business, as they seek to gather ever more of the nectar of wealth. Not for them pure, unadulterated foods, but the easily available, fast food of today. It is ironic how quickly fast foods slow you down!

Sugar needs are often met in the relaxing, end-of-day drink, a glass of wine, or the traditional whiskey, or a glass of cola. The fat comes in the form of the best steak

- lean red meat is about forty percent fat - or chicken, in cakes and pastries, in caviar and chocolate, to name just a few. And none of this a crime; it is simply cause, and all cause reaps an effect.

If you see yourself in any of this, and you feel inner alarm, heed the prompting. You may continue as a hunter of wealth, but please, look upon soul-self as a more worthy cause. Hunt also for your health. Learn about nutrition. And instead of simply accepting the medical research financed by the corporate drug companies, look far deeper into the issues of human health, where the corrupted tentacles of vested interests have not yet reached.

MOVIE SNACKS

The wealthy are not by any means the only unhealthy people in our society. And, oddly, once the message really sinks in, many of the wealthy are more likely to do something positive to improve their health.

Have you been to the cinema lately? Did you load up with a sugar-laden drink, or an ice cream, or a large container of popcorn? On a subconscious level, your body/brain knows that you are going into an emotional experience, reacting with a craving for fat and sugar. Let's face it, if there were no emotional thrills, scares, tears, and laughs, the highs and lows, you would not go to the movies. The cinema industry is well aware of the connection between emotions and their related cravings, and this is catered for. This is good for the movie industry's profits, but it is not good for your health. The continuous habit of movie snacks, along with your daily fat and sugar - the burger and cola - have a far higher price than your initial cost. You pay with your health, your life. Meaning, when those years down the track have passed, your family has grown, and sickness becomes a permanent visitor, you pay with emotional and mental anguish, not to mention the physical suffering involved. Your children, and those who love you, will also pay a high emotional price for your neglect of your overall health. This is not an experience of true prosperity! Again, this is all your choice, but if you have any intention toward true prosperity then you have to live what you learn. The inappropriate food habits must be put aside, and proper nutrition allowed its place in your life. Any good nutritionist will tell you that just about every disease you are likely to get can be prevented by eating in a way that supports your physical health, rather than attacks it. Not surprisingly, the nutrition that supports your physical health, is also the best support for your emotional and mental well-being.

ISSUE IN THE TISSUE

I have a Danish friend who is a body worker. His favourite saying comes when he talks about, 'the issue in the tissue.' Sounds odd, but his words are succinctly sound. Any issue we have in life - mental or emotional - gets imbedded into the physical tissue of the body. Not only that, but this issue is carried by consciousness from one frame of your life-movie to another, to once again become re-established in the tissue. Another of the Principles of Truth explains it well: Consciousness draws to self physical form through which to express, and the expression is consciousness. Discord in consciousness means discord in the physical.

Deal with your issues. Face what needs to be faced, and do what you need to do to resolve it. Unresolved issues adversely affect your health. Remember: Anything in the past which is unresolved, is unresolved now. Of course, none of this is conventional thinking. This is not a conventional book! Bring your life into order. Treat your body as though it has been given to you as a sacred trust. It has. Treat your body with respect, rather than the contempt of neglect. Consider your good health as the greatest benefit you have. And if you do not have good health, then seek to get it back with focus and intent. Hold in mind that you threw it away, and it is up to you to get it back and keep it!

A COMMON COMMENT

You will remember earlier I mentioned dropping the negative, "I can't afford" from your thinking and speaking, and replacing it with, "Plenty more where this comes from." There is another one of those common, everyday comments that has a nasty negative effect on your health and lifestyle. Remember, we live our conversations.

Treenie and I both do weight training three times a week at a fitness centre. We give a lot of focus toward achieving perfect health, and we both consider we are fitter now than we have ever been. When we first joined, there was a period of getting to know the regulars, an exchange of names, and the usual Oz greetings, "G'day Michael, how are you?" To which I would reply, "I'm really well, thanks."

I then asked, "And how are you?" Almost without exception the reply was, "Not bad." This posed a dilemma for me. It was the wrong answer! If I care enough about a person to ask about the state of their Being - "How are you?" - and they give me a reply that will consistently reduce the quality of their life, then what do I do? Ignore it, or explain their comment to them? I chose to explain it.

REACTION AND RESPONSE

I asked one guy, a body builder, what he meant by "Not bad." Did it mean, 'I could be worse,' or did it mean, 'Not quite bad,' or 'I could be better,' or 'halfway good,' or what? He looked at me with an expression of utter astonishment. He scowled, smiled, and did not know what to say. So I explained to him that words are powerful. I told him that the mind discards some words, while using others as a focus. I said, "When you say, 'not bad,' the mind discards a word like 'not,' and 'bad' becomes the focus. And what you focus the mind on, it will manifest." I told him that saying, "Not bad," will lead to the point where he will eventually be saying, "I'm really sick." I suggested that when asked, "How are you?" he reply either, "Half good," or "Really good." I told him that if the focus word is 'good,' then good is where you are heading. As I told him, good health is far more pleasant to experience than bad.

Without going into any more detail, I caringly explained this to several men. Without exception, they all reacted in different ways. Put simply, for the next month or so, they made sure of minimal exchange between us! One of them good naturedly 'kidded me' while another seemed to understand and go along with it. I decided that all in all, although I was true to myself, it would have been better to have said nothing. Better to simply say, "G'day," and leave it at that.

Quite a few months passed, and it seemed to gradually be forgotten. The man who had 'kidded me' always replied to my greeting that he was "Really good." One of the men slowly built up anger, and told me off one day for being arrogant. This came about mainly because when he asked me, "What have you been up too?" I jokingly replied, "Great deeds." He is used to the usual self-deprecating humour, not self-elevating humour. Fair enough. I had also been trying to encourage him to stop smoking, and to improve his overall fitness. He reacted, saying that his 'real' friends accepted him the way he is. I tried to encourage him to reach his potential - but he had not asked for this. He was right. No matter how good my intention, I was out of line.

REALLY GOOD

Eventually, Treenie and I were absent from the gym for three-and-a-half months while we were traveling overseas on our annual five-day Retreat and Seminar tour. When we returned, the body builder was telling me how he had got his life together, and that things had never been better for him. I was delighted. After his initial embarrassment with me, and keeping his distance, he had always replied to my greeting with, "I'm getting better all the time." I would reply, "That's just great." His life improved with his words and focus, and he realises this. I get great pleasure from somebody getting their life together.

However, I have to admit, people who reply, 'not bad' to my greeting now, will just have to live with it! The point between 'good intentions' and 'interfering' is too close.

The point of my story is, of course, are you a 'not bad' person? If so, it will take you well away from true prosperity. 'Not bad' is a downhill track into 'much worse.' I encourage you to always speak positively about yourself and your health. Throw 'not bad' away, and embrace, 'really good.' Speak yourself up, not down. Never put yourself down with your words, because if you do, others will. If you talk poorly of yourself, or about being financially 'hard up' your conversation will maintain it. Never be self-deprecating in your conversation. Always be self-elevating, speaking of yourself as worthy of respect and admiration. If people in your life cannot deal with this, let them go from your life. You cannot learn to swim while attached to a heavy weight.

THERE IS FOOD – AND THERE IS FOOD!

In Oz, one in four people over the age of twenty-five have diabetes. In North America diabetes has increased by as much as 600% in one generation. Type 2 diabetes is practically always caused by food, yet it can also be cured by food. This poses a question. How much of what you eat is *really* food? Food, according to my modern dictionary, is "any substance that can be ingested and metabolised into energy and tissue." A diet of junk food and drink will meet this definition, but it will also lead you to an early death. We need a lot more intelligence than that in our definition of food. However, my *Chambers Mid-Century* (20th) *Dictionary* states, "food; that which, being digested, brings nourishment to the body." This is very different. Further investigation provides more insight. Both dictionaries agree that to nourish means; to provide with the materials necessary for life and growth. And thus we get to - life. Food is, or should be, about sustaining life. Cooked food is life destroying, not life sustaining.

It may not please you to read this, you may react. All nature gets its nourishment from raw food. Raw food is living food. Even the vulture eats living food, for although the spirit has left the animal, its flesh is alive with bacteria and enzymes. By contrast, cooked food is dead food. All life in the food is destroyed, enzymes, bacteria, everything. Also lost is the 'life force' of the plant, grain, or animal. The field of 'light energy' is destroyed, denied to any person who eats cooked food. As physical Beings we take energy from the substance of food, while as spiritual Beings we also take nourishment from the 'life force' of food. When one of these factors is missing, we are seriously imbalanced. The result is inner discord, leading to a vast multitude of sicknesses, and premature death.

SIX GOLDEN RULES

If you did react to what you just read, be aware of what this means. If your reaction was positive, then you are open to change, and can move ahead. If your reaction was negative, then you are attached to the way things are for you, and you will progress accordingly. Treenie eats about 80-90 percent raw food, and is vibrant and healthy. When I try this, I get seriously underweight and weak. I eat rolled oats and rolled barley or fruit for breakfast, depending on what type of work I will be doing that day. Generally, raw fruit is my evening meal, while lunch is raw or cooked food according to circumstances. I am strong, energised, and healthy. Okay, my Six Golden Rules of Health.

1) Overeating leads you toward sickness, disease, and premature death. Undereating leads you toward excellent health, high vitality, and longevity. Stop eating before you feel full.

2) Eat food that supports and nourishes your body,

not junk food and drink that attack it.

3) Food should be eaten with an aware appreciation, not with TV, a video, or a newspaper.

4) Your thoughts and your food are linked. Supportive thinking leads to supportive eating.

5) If you eat in a way that supports nature and life, then life will also support you.

6) The joy in eating good food is food for the soul. Joy is a powerful, uplifting energy.

Summary

True prosperity embraces complete health and happiness. I would never claim that happiness is impossible without full health, for happiness is an inner expression of the spirit, but believe me, it certainly helps. And by full health I mean spiritual, emotional, and mental health, as well as physical. Maximising your raw food intake empowers you on every level of your Being, and in more ways than simply nutritional. It is said that you are what you eat. I disagree. You are more the result of your thinking than the food you ingest. However, what you eat will seriously affect your thinking, and what you think will have a dramatic affect on your choice of food, so there is a strong connection. I encourage you to explore every avenue of food and exercise that you can. Find out what works best for you. The price of inattention to your body and health is very high, and you pay with far more than money.

There are many books available on the subject of food and nutrition, mostly with strongly opposing views and opinions. Read and learn, but use your own intuition and body as the guide that leads you to premium health. Life is always about choices, but we have to live the results of those choices. You have a choice now. Are you going to eventually be another 'person in hospital' statistic, or are you going to take back your health by accepting that you, and you only, are responsible for it? If you allow it to happen, your body has a miraculous program of bio-logical self-healing. Raw food switches the program full on, too much cooked food and the program is drastically impaired. Try it. Give yourself an opportunity to climb out of the sickness industry and into a life of vibrant health. You can do it!

A full and benevolent heart is the birthplace of abundance.

11   ASPECTS OF ABUNDANCE

Awake, or waking sleep?

Everyday living quickly reveals where you are at in life. That is, of course, if you are taking any notice. Most people are not. It hurts me to know that a great number of people's lives are simply functional existence, rather than dynamic and creative. So many people do the same things day in and day out, year after year, with no thought about why they do what they do. I was one of those people. I did not ask myself why I did what I did, even though I did not like it. Why? Because I did not want to hear the answer. To be honest, I did not even want to hear the question! This is living in a dream world. We believe that we wake up after a night's sleep; but do we? Do you? Or do you dream that you are awake and go through your day in the illusions of that dream. This, for most people, is life.

How is it possible to experience true prosperity or abundance while living like this? Is your life abundant? Do you realise that 'all' your experiences are empowering you, so that you gain by them? Are you aware of the miracle of life that you are? Do you honour and nourish that miracle in everyday life? When someone you love dies, do you ever think, what happened? What was it that departed from their body? What is this quintessential essence of self that is life? Right now, within you is this incredible divine spark of 'life force.' Why not honour it? Do you think about yourself as a magnificent Being, and all that this implies? Or, do you give little thought or focus toward the miracle you are, on the life force you contain, on how magnificent you truly are?

OPEN THE DOORS

If you are unaware of your divinity, of your magnificence, of the miracle that you are, then these are not flourishing in your life. I hope that you realise this. An hour ago, while I was writing this book, I felt such happiness that I went upstairs and, picking up my youngest granddaughter, Jacinta, I swung her round and around, hugging her. I could feel the abundance of life thrumming and drumming inside me so powerfully that I had to share it. I hugged Jaspher, my oldest grandson, and in our hugging my happiness just kept on growing. What triggered such happiness? Life, the moment, and consciously being in it. That is all it takes. Nothing else is needed.

All you have to do is open the doors. Certainly it helps if you are vitally healthy in the moment. Certainly it helps if you are aware of the sheer abundance that your life is, and the miracle that you are, and it also helps if you feel overwhelming appreciation and gratitude for all this. But these, of course, are the ways of opening the doors!

ARE YOU IN YOUR HEART?

What does the dictionary have to say about abundance? Surprise, surprise! *The Mid-Century* (20th) *Dictionary* says: "ample sufficiency, great plenty," while the modern version states: "copious supply; fullness or benevolence, from the abundance of my heart." And there we have it; a full and benevolent heart is the birthplace of abundance. This brings up a question. Are you in your heart, or is your heart simply in you? Do you feel in your heart a fullness and benevolence for yourself? Do you regard yourself with compassion and love?

This is what a rich, full, and abundant life is all about. Regarding yourself and life with judgment and criticism is the birthplace of cynicism and mediocrity. A full and benevolent heart is the birthplace of abundance. Which do you choose? And remember, only by living your choice have you made a choice.

I know that there are people who, having heard

me speak in public, have regarded me with suspicion and cynicism. The words and energy of their thoughts have been negative, but only to them, never to me. You own your thoughts, and you have no choice but to own and experience their energy. Equally, the majority of listeners who have thought of me with respect and high regard also get to experience that energy for themselves. Our every thought, our every moment, is creative and creating. Even the people I mentioned earlier as simply functioning are creative, but only in as much as they are creating more of the same.

FOOD CHAINS

When Treenie and I were in America quite a few years ago, we were taken out to have lunch in town. To my surprise our host took us to one of the cheaper food-chain restaurants, so we had to wait in a queue at the service counter. When I told the server behind the glass display counter that I wanted some food from one side of the glass partition, and some from the other. She told me that this was not possible. "Why not?" I asked.

"Because the food is on different sides of the partition," she replied wearily.

"But you can easily reach in with one hand on each side and take what I want."

"I can't do that," she scowled. "Each side is a different price."

"That's okay," I smiled. "Just put it all on the plate. The cash desk will add it up."

She looked at me as though I was crazy. "They can't do that. Just choose one side or the other, sir, that's the way we do things around here."

Our host was listening to all this, and regarding me with some surprise. He could see that I was being deliberately provocative. My choice made, I continued through the process.

FOOD FOR THOUGHT

Sitting at our table, on plastic chairs that matched the food, our host and I looked at each other. "So what was that all about?" he asked.

"Do you have a money problem?" I countered.

For a few moments he huffed and puffed, then admitted that he did.

"Do you eat here on a regular basis?" I asked.

Frowning, he nodded.

"I presume that you eat at this cheap place because you have a money problem."

With some embarrassment, he affirmed that this was so.

"Has it ever occurred to you that the reverse could be true? That you have a money problem because you eat here. Look around you, look at the food. Is there any quality in any of this? It's all cheap and nasty. Poor quality everything. Now, this is neither good nor bad, not right nor wrong, but it is a powerful statement in your daily life. "

"What are you getting at?" he asked defensively.

"I'm saying that on a regular basis you make the statement by eating here that you and cheap and nasty fit together, and that cheap and nasty is good enough for you. You are putting the message into consciousness, that you, through your own self-evaluation, deserve cheap and nasty. How do you expect a good financial flow in that framework?"

THE FOOD OF RESPECT

He looked shocked. "My God! I've never thought about it like that before."

"Everything you do, every action, every thought, is building your life," I told him. "Every thought is either weaving abundance or poverty into your life. Personally, I'll never eat here again. It does not honour me. I suggest that you look for a place that has really good food, and good energy, and eat there. It certainly will not be the cheapest place, but neither need it be very expensive. It is not about the cost, it's about the energy of the place, the food, the service . . . and you. If you eat at a place where they have respect for their food, along with a respect for their staff and customers, then you are nurturing self-respect in you every time you eat there."

"So you made that fuss in there just to teach me a lesson?"

I nodded, grinning. "We cosmic teachers have to use whatever's appropriate and available!"

Hopefully, he took the lesson to heart. The story illustrates my point, it is not possible to have abundance if you treat yourself as being poor. The first stage of poverty is in thinking poor. If a child born into, and surrounded by poverty manages to think only of abundance, then that will become the reality of their life. Not probably or maybe, but definitely. Equally, the reverse can happen. If you were to suddenly inherit wealth but you continued with poverty thinking, then the scenario can split. You may invest the wealth in a way that maintains and even increases it, but your physical and emotional health will spiral downward. Your poverty thinking will become far more personalised. Poverty thinking is self-punishment. I repeat, wealth alone is not true prosperity.

DISCOUNTING SELF

There are many other examples of thinking from a poverty 'I can't afford' attitude. Let us go back to the shops. Do you rush to get to the 'end-of-year' sales? Or the 'mid-year' sales, or the 'closing down' sales? In Oz, people fight each other to get to the counter to buy something - anything - simply because it is a bargain. Surveys have shown that more than half the people at these sales buy items that either do not fit, or they do not really want. Why? Because the items are cheap, and the people have an 'I can't afford' program running their lives. Again, the message in consciousness is that I need to buy cheap because money is tight.

Some of you might be thinking, 'But money *is* tight, that's why I go!' Just the thought, 'but money *is* tight' is all it takes to perpetuate the situation. And money will be tight. This is not about money, it is about you. True prosperity is a state of consciousness. The physical, daily game of life simply demonstrates and expresses what is taking place in your consciousness.

Consider it this way; first there is you, then comes your thinking. As you grow older, your thinking will begin to manifest itself in your daily life. This will last for as long as you live. Some people make huge amounts of money in their lifetime, this is what they most focus on. They are playing money games. Some people use that money to gather power to themselves, they are playing power games. Some people become wealthy movie stars, or capture the media attention for most of their lives, they are playing fame games. Some people spend all their lives following their version of the word of God, they are playing religion games. And so it continues, there are many, many games.

THE GAME OF LIFE

We all play our games, and nobody should judge the rights or wrongs of these games. They are our life. However, if, during your life, you experience many years of love, fulfillment, and happiness, with a feeling of joy in your heart, then you can be sure that you are playing the right game for you. You are experiencing true prosperity, and that is wonderful.

If, however, you are not having this positive, uplifting experience, then your life is showing you that you are playing the wrong game. Change it! This book is about changing your game. What I am sharing in the pages of this book will put you in the very centre of the game of life. And it is a *great* game. The game of life is about you. You play the game with power tools. Not electric power tools, but the human tools of power; love, appreciation, respect, confidence, honour, and openness. This opens the doors to income and abundance, to order and balance, to happiness and fulfilment.

Of course, there are many more power tools, and you will use the ones that are most appropriate to you, but they do need to be used. Every day, all day, you are either building quality and abundance into your life, or you are emptying it out.

NEVER STATIC

There is no static place in your life. In every moment of your life abundance is either increasing or decreasing. Love is either growing daily in your life, or it is receding. Nothing stays the same. As I have said, you can create sameness in your life, where nothing ever seems to vary and everything seems to be the same, but in reality it is a downhill slide into increasing negativity, into lack, into blame. You may not be aware of this in a single frame of the movie of your life, but if you look at the bigger picture, it becomes very apparent.

Nature demonstrates this principle beautifully. If you focus a video camera on a flower and leave it running for a day, then condense the film into one hour, you will have visual evidence of the continuous, never ending movement of the flower. If you were to do the same with a rock, nothing would appear to change. However, if you took a year of filming and condensed it into an hour, you would see the surface of the rock appear to move. Life is about expansion and growth, contraction and decay. This is your choice. Expansion and growth, or contraction and decay. And remember, whole societies, whole cities, whole nations of people have contracted and decayed into nothing.

FUEL FOR THOUGHT

As I travel around, I see many signs of abundance thinking or poverty thinking. Some people have a fear of spending money on themselves - lack of self-worth - but will freely spend on other people. Others will spend a lot of money on themselves, but grudge spending money on other people. This is the same lack of self-worth! Dictated by the program of our personal fears, we express our lack in many different ways!

When Treenie and I are overseas, and we are being driven around, I often take notice of the petrol gauge in their car. Some people run their car constantly in the top half of the fuel tank. As soon as the fuel gauge dips below half, they stop at a petrol station and fill the car. These people like safety and security, and they like the feeling of 'plenty' in their life. Some people always run their car in the lower half of the petrol tank, often running precariously close to empty. These people are inclined to live their life with frugality, mostly having the 'I can't afford' syndrome. Even when they fill up the petrol tank, they only half fill it. I had an uncle who would often run out of petrol, rather than fill the petrol tank. He then used to curse the inconvenience, and somehow, it was always someone else's fault!

It all indicates the differences in people. There are those people who see how 'much' there is in life, while others see how 'little' there is. And the way you see it, is the way it is.

PASSION IN ACTION

One of the great keys to freeing up abundance is your passion. Consider me. I have a great passion for sharing Truth, both writing it and speaking it. I also have a great passion for my garden, and growing exotic plants in a tropical house. So I indulge my passions, and by doing so I am expressing my creativity. Now, let us suppose that you have a great passion for making money. This is wonderful. However, many people on their spiritual path feel guilty about this, thinking that their passion should only be for spiritual matters.

Tropical plants express a type of energy, money expresses a type of energy. Neither is right nor wrong, good nor bad. You can, of course, think that plants are good and money is bad, but only your thoughts have created this belief, and only your life will be affected by those thoughts. If you have a passion for growing plants, go for it. If you have a passion for making money, go for it. We each have our passions for a reason, and properly focused your passion is your passport to a full and abundant life. It is up to you to use the passport.

Spiritual money

Making money can be just as spiritual as gardening. If the gardeners are attached to their plants, and receive no real joy in sharing the abundance of the earth, then they have no spiritual connection with the earth or the plants. Equally, if the money-makers are attached to their money, and receive no real joy from sharing their abundance, then there is no spiritual connection with making money.

If, however, both the gardener and the money-maker feel passion and joy in what they are doing, if they feel enthusiasm and even excitement, then they are united in their spiritual connection with life. One is growing plants, the other is growing money. Each expression is as truly spiritual as the other, as long as they are free from attachment to either the plants or the money.

Attachments are the bindings and trappings of fear. Attachment severs all spiritual connection between self and where you are expressing your focus and energy. I have mentioned the term, the trappings of success. Whether you are attached to plants or money, you are trapped. Your attachment is like a pair of handcuffs holding you firmly anchored, disconnected from the spiritual freedom that life offers. This is often described as success!

HOME LOAN, OR RENT?

If making money is your passion, please, do not feel guilty. Give freedom to your passion, freely spread your money around, and enjoy. If you maintain a spiritual focus, honouring self and other people, seeing the divine in all life, you are on your spiritual path.

Abundance is living in the credit side of life. Very many people live on the debit side. If you live in a state of debt it is difficult to feel abundant. Young people who get married in today's society are compelled to take out a huge loan if they wish to purchase a house. In Oz this is not difficult, even though the repayment can be a twenty-year burden. In some countries land and housing is so very expensive that the financial burden is not possible, and the young couple become lifetime rent payers.

People are very different. Some can easily handle the loan repayment, psychologically as well as financially, while others, even having the finances, are very stressed by long-term loans. Renting or purchasing is not of great importance, unless you strongly prefer one or the other. What is important is that you take on a financial structure that enables you, personally, to feel abundant in life, and to be aware of the abundance around you. This connection with abundance is a very important factor in your true prosperity. If you do not *feel* abundance, it is impossible to attract it.

ABUNDANCE SYMBOL

I recommend that you find an abundance symbol in your life. Just as with a computer you use an icon to bring up the program you want, so an abundance symbol can have a similar effect. In the early 1990's Treenie and I were on route to America. We were rather shaky in our financial resources, and a bit uncertain if we should even be going to America. Treenie looked out the aircraft window and saw a wonderful sight. A perfect sphere of brilliant, double rainbow light was hovering just above the wing tip. In the clear centre of the sphere, surrounded by the colour, was a miniaturised reflection of our aircraft. She drew my attention and we both gazed at it, spellbound. Two minutes passed before it gradually faded away. We knew then that all was well . . . and so it proved to be. Ever since then the rainbow has been our symbol of abundance. When we extended our house in the late 1990's, we had to have a bulldozer tear into a portion of our hill. The earth seemed so devastated by this that I felt uneasy about it. Early next morning, well before work recommenced, a strong rainbow arced over the building site, and I knew all was well. The abundance and well-being of our home and garden was being enhanced and empowered by our work, not reduced.

SUMMARY

You were born in an abundant universe, on an abundant world. Abundance is your birthright, but you have to claim it. Just as a deceased person's last will and testament may require that all who have a claim on the inheritance should come forward and make that claim, so you have to step forward and make a clear and definite claim on abundance.

Abundance is a responsive energy. You can claim your birthright, and attract it toward you, you can ignore it, or you can dismiss it, repelling it from your life. It is your choice. But, again I draw your attention to the fact that it is your thoughts, words, and attitude that attract, ignore, or repel abundance. Wealth is not abundance, for abundance cannot be limited to a single manifestation. Wealth, however, can be part of your abundance, part of the overall richness that empowers and fills your life.

You can have overflowing abundance, while your neighbour experiences poverty and hardship. You cannot give them abundance, nor can it be stolen from you. If you lost everything you owned and possessed, but the feeling of abundance remained strongly within you, untouched by material loss, then your life would quickly be refilled to overflowing.

Thoughts that are self-honouring uplift and fulfill you, leading you toward true prosperity.

12 TO HONOUR YOURSELF

YOUR JUST DESERTS!

Let us once again refer to the modern dictionary for the meaning of honour: "Personal integrity; allegiance to moral principles." The *Chambers Mid-Century* (20th) *Dictionary* is much more explicit: "The esteem due or paid to worth; self-respect and esteem;" and, after a long list, "a fine and scrupulous sense of what is your due." I like that. Due means something justly deserved. So, in effect, to honour yourself is to treat yourself with self-respect, to live with personal integrity, and to be keenly aware that you 'justly deserve' the rewards of your life.

The days of your life are the playing fields of self-expression. Honour is a soul expression, rather than purely personal. However misunderstood, every Awakened soul expresses honourably, even if the personality expression may seem dubious. If you live in a way of honouring self, you are uniting personal integrity with soul expression, and you become wholistically empowered in the process.

Living with honour is something you do from the moment the idea unfolds within you until the so-called end of your life. Living with honour is a commitment; a start-to-finish commitment which, to the best of your ability, is expressed in everything you do.

Honouring self

Despite having mentioned a start-to-finish commitment, there are many personal dilemmas that can appear, muddying the clarity. I once committed myself to giving a one-day seminar in mid-winter in Oz. When Treenie and I arrived the location was in the deep shade of a mountain, the venue a rotunda with see-through gaps in the walls, and louvre windows. Ice coated the insides of the windows, and the interior was freezing. The people who attended were on a spiritual retreat, and no heating was offered. They sat wrapped in blankets. I miserably endured that freezing day (it thawed late afternoon) because of my commitment.

Later, I realised that the people owning the venue did not honour themselves, or Treenie and I. The conditions were appalling. Today, I would walk out.

Quite a few years later, I was asked to give a talk on organic growing at a university venue in the U.S. When we arrived we were met by the organisers at an outside venue where hundreds of students milled around dozens of tables forming three sides of a huge square. Each table was promoting and espousing their cause; Greenpeace, Amnesty International, Save the Dolphins, etc. On the open side was a stage, with a band busily setting themselves up. I learned that I was expected to stand on the platform and, ignoring the noise behind me, and the hubbub of the students before me, talk through the microphone to any of the students who would care to listen.

I refused. I told them that my words have value. If people were sitting, ready to listen, I would happily speak. But there was no way that I was going to cast my words into a busy, noisy crowd of students in the hopes that some of them might listen. This neither honoured me, nor the value and worth of what I had to say.

Despite being unhappy about it, the organisers considered they learned more about self-worth and integrity by that action, than if I had spoken. In any situation only you can decide what is honouring for you, and what is demeaning. Honour is not about what is right or wrong, or about meeting other people's expectations, it is about you in the moment.

Honouring emotions

In your everyday life, honour your thinking. Be aware that if your thoughts become aggressive, or hostile, or cynical, or any other of the negatives, then that is what you are bringing into *your* life. Not the life of the person or people you are thinking about, but *your* life. Thoughts lead to actions. Thoughts precede emotions. A lot of people are highly emotional, some almost uncontrollably so. Apart from a recent bereavement, it is difficult to get emotional without conjuring up the thoughts that lead to the emotion. Grieving death, or loss, is natural and desirable, but emotions have their time. A continued emotional focus is debilitating and destabilising, honouring neither the person or people involved, nor does it honour you. Healthy emotions are 'in the moment,' and balanced. All this requires is the thought process to lead you into areas of appreciation and anticipation. Appreciate the qualities and memories of the past, while anticipating the highest potential of your future.

Thoughts that are self-honouring uplift and fulfill you, leading you toward true prosperity. These are the thoughts that attract the type of people whom you want and need in your life, people who accept that honouring self is a rare and noble quality. If you accept that there is nothing outside of Self, how can you honour nature or humanity if you do not honour self? The very birthplace of this honour is in the quality of your thoughts about self.

HONOURING ACTIONS

Thoughts lead to actions. Thoughts are an energy, while your actions are a physical expression of that energy. Live in a way that you can honour your actions. So many people take impulsive action that they later regret. All that was required was some rational thought preceding the action, rather than rash or angry thoughts that lead to trouble and disaster. The majority of murders are committed from angry thoughts leading to overcharged emotions, followed by lethal action. The prison cell has offered thousands of people time to reflect on the rash, out-of-control moment that ruined their life.

We all do and say things that we regret. This is part of being human, but we can also improve on our performance, thinking thoughts that lead to kind action, and high self-regard. People with high self-esteem live with a lot less regretted moments than the people who dislike themselves. Ask yourself, which group are you in, and which you would prefer? And remember, you have to live your choice! This is essential for true prosperity.

HONOUR IN THE WORKPLACE

I have often heard men on various work sites talking to each other in derogatory terms, much of the time saying things to each other that they did not really mean. Although this is meant to be humour, it neither honours your fellow workers, nor yourself. Nor does it honour your words. Spoken words are vehicles of power; the power to hurt, ridicule, or uplift. Any words that you speak that are not empowering for others, are disempowering for them - and you. No matter how harmless the intent, or how funny it may seem, cause is sown and the eventual harvest is distress. In the huge corporations, where people work enmasse at desks and computers, stress is an ever accompanying factor. Just the stress of constant high frequency electronic energy is enough to be debilitating, without discord among the people. Do not be one of the people who speaks negatively about others, or indulge in destructive office gossip. When you are not supportive of other people, you have lost your honour.

HONOUR YOUR HOME

Home has different meanings for different people. For me, home is being with my beloved Treenie, on our hectare of tree-filled land with a beautiful house and garden. I am extremely fortunate, and deeply honour all that I have. I do this by keeping the house fully maintained, the garden a place of beauty and vibrant energy, and appreciating every moment spent with my wife. Fortunate, I am, but luck has nothing to do with it. We each create our own reality, and Treenie and I have created one of true prosperity for ourselves.

I honour my house, and every room within it. In this way, the house and rooms honour me. Do you see the dynamics of this? As I have often stated, all life is energy. This energy forms the essence of all natural substances, including the structure and materials of your house. Equally, the personal integrity and self-respect of your honour is also an expression of energy. When you honour self, and you honour your home, these energies blend into one wholistic expression, a vibration that uplifts and empowers the people in such a residence. I can feel this energy when I enter such a house, just as I can feel the very different energy in a household where there is anger and continuous arguments.

HONOUR YOUR PARTNER

One of the greatest gifts that life can bestow upon you is to have a family. To have a partner in life who truly loves you . . . is priceless. So often, when people are under pressure they take their frustrations out on the people who are closest to them. Does that make sense? Especially when the family has nothing to do with the reasons for being pressured. How much more sensible to declare the family and home a 'zone of peace.' Talk it over with your partner. Both of you make a decision that all pressures, anger, and frustrations shall not be inflicted on the person and people whom you most love, the ones who are closest to you. The problems can be discussed in a supportive atmosphere, and answers found. There is no need to fight, creating more tension, violence, and the torment of deep regret and guilt.

You may well be thinking, what about rows between couples? I suggest that instead of spending angry time arguing over your differences and disagreements, you spend time in a more valuable way. Try spending more relaxed time focussed on everything that you agree about, and all that is mutually supportive. True prosperity has never come from arguments, or infidelity, or anything that does less than honour your partner and yourself.

Far too many couples focus on their problems, however small, eventually creating mountains out of molehills. Reverse this, creating a mountain out of all that you agree on, while your disagreements dwindle to nothing from sheer neglect.

Honour your children

Every animal in nature sets boundaries and limits for their offspring. The young are strictly disciplined. Without this as a foundation, the young would die soon after leaving their parents. Of course there are exceptions in nature, but mostly, this is the way it happens. We, as a species, need no less. In our present times, it seems the current trend is letting children have their own way while offering no true discipline. School teachers can be sued for even mild physical discipline. And the invariable result is negative. I am not talking here of physical beatings or abuse, I am talking of normal, sensible, appropriate discipline. There are many meanings to the word discipline, I am using it to mean 'guidelines and boundaries.' This does not mean continual threats, or a litany of shouted NO's. Threats with no follow-up action (such as grounded for a week) are seriously detrimental, besides eroding all respect for the parent. Gentle but firm is a good standard for discipline.

Without discipline there is no way that you can honour your children. I have found that in all the families of my youth, the kids who were most disciplined by their parents are the ones who remained closest to their parents when they became adults. Obviously, as a adult you will only be close to your parents if the dicipline was appropriate and a bonding took place between you, or, if you even want to be close to them. I value the closeness I share with my children, probably because I did not feel such a strong bond with my parents. By your caring, sensible and reasonable discipline you honour your children, paving the way for the establishment of their self-esteem. And this is a prerequisite for their future prosperity.

HONOUR YOUR EXCELLENCE

The people who stand out from the crowd all share one common factor; they have a close relationship with excellence. They set out to become the best, to excel! They all make a personal commitment of endeavour to achieve their dreams, be it sport, art, acting, business, whatever. As already stated, people in Oz like to cut down tall poppies, yet tall poppies are the very people who embody excellence. Of course, excellence will not necessarily make you likeable, or improve your personality, but it is a necessary ingredient for high achievement.

Consider then, excellence in self: expressing in your daily life, in love and marriage, in child raising, in attaining true prosperity and abundance, in being a person whom others honour and respect. What better expression for excellence? Rarely are there any public accolades, but you get plenty of private and personal ones. To know that your spouse or partner looks at you with pride, and deeply respects and loves you, honouring your finer qualities . . . priceless. To know that your children love, honour and respect you, and that you learned it and earned it . . . rare and priceless.

Bring excellence into your life. Do it effortlessly, not as another burden. Just be the best that you can be, all the time. Use excellence as a focus, a way to honour yourself.

HONOURING LOVE AND LIFE

Sadly, a deep and committed love is not common in marriages or partnerships. All too often love is conditional. We use the word 'love' carelessly, "Oh, I love my new car." Is that the true meaning of love? Such a comment devalues the real meaning of love. Many movies revolve around the theme of love, exploring its many different interpretations and expressions. More often than not they romanticise it. True love is unconditional. Not, I love you if you love me. Think about this for a few moments - your love for another person with absolutely no conditions attached. This is rare!

It is said and written that around two thousand years ago a Great Teacher came to teach us about unconditional love. We must be incredibly slow learners. We actually have world leaders who believe that you can fight for peace! Did that Great Teacher suggest that we fight our neighbours, or violate other nations, or add more terror to terrorism? Yet today, a few world leaders promote 'might is right' in the name of that Teacher.

You may think, 'not much I can do about that.' Wrong. You can! You can do plenty. Remember energy fields? The strongest and most powerful energy on this planet is love. If you are living in a way that you are honouring love, by living and expressing love, you affect all humanity, you affect the world. We attract and magnify all that we focus on. Your energy field combines with, and empowers, the universal energy field of love on this, our planet. If your focus is love, and if you express love in your daily life, you are generating and expressing the most powerful force for human upliftment and positive change on this planet. You are sowing the seeds of true prosperity across all humanity.

HONOUR YOUR BODY

Recently I was talking to a woman who is depressed and confused. Her long term goal had been to be financially independent for life, now, suddenly, she is. Although her situation has changed, it has resolved nothing for her as a person. During our conversation I asked her if she could stand naked in front of the bath-room mirror and love her body as it is. "No way," she said. "I hate my body." Okay, her body is overweight, and she wants it slim, but her attitude to her body is dangerous to her health. A body that is hated, constantly criticised, is a body getting the focus of self-attack; this is a sickness focus. It results in cancer, heart disease, and other manifestations of self-attack. In a U.S. survey, two thousand women were asked whether or not they considered their breasts as perfect. Apparently, not one woman accepted them as perfect. Not one! That is scary. Constant thoughts of criticism of your breasts is the birthplace of breast cancer. Discord creates dis-ease.

How can you even begin any form of self-honour if you hate your body or any part of it? You need to realise that your body is a product of your choices, your lifestyle. And only you can change it. First and foremost, you be-gin by acknowledging that if your body is not as you want it, then you must accept responsibility for it. You then honour your body by embracing and applying the neces-sary lifestyle changes that will result in a slimmer, fitter body that you can love and accept. And plastic surgery will not do this. Once the effects reach their 'use by' date, the problem reoccurs. And reoccurs. And . . .

This body is yours, it needs to be loved and honoured. Since Treenie and I began at the fitness centre we have regained lost strength, body flexibility, and overall fitness. Every second week we have a deep body massage - and the body loves it. Truly honouring!

Honour your soul

Sadly, for some people this is no more than a remote concept. As I have written earlier, you are an eternal Being. You are a Being of soul, the quintessential Self. This is the aspect of you that continues from one frame of the 'Continuity of Self' movie to another. You live in the illusion that you are the identity of your birth name, but this is not who you are. You are a soul Being. Some of you reading this will know what I mean, others will not, but this does not really matter. Truth has its timing. Let us simply say that essentially, you are a Being of Light. For the sake of this analogy, let us say that this Light is easily stained. Negative thoughts and actions leave deep lingering stains in the Light body, and those stains are detrimental to you. They throw shadows onto the Playing Fields of Life. These stains are in your soul. Yet, the stains are not indelible. You can live in such a way that your 'love in action' can gradually erase them. By honouring yourself, and by living within a framework of consideration and respect for other people, you can remove all the stains from your body of Light. Unknown to you, in many frames of your life-movie you have both added and removed stains, over and over, all unaware of the repercussions of your daily actions. Now, with focus and intent, you can consciously remove stains by honouring your soul.

HONOUR YOUR INTELLIGENCE

Any intelligent person knows that if you have a heavy boulder that is impossible for you to move, an iron bar and a fulcrum will enable you to move a weight that was previously unmovable. A fulcrum is the pivot which creates the leverage. It is also defined as something that supports and sustains. So let us suppose that *you* are the heavy boulder, burdened with the many little responsibilities in your life, all of which add up to a heavy weight. Let us also suppose that the fulcrum is made of love and trust. This means that love and trust is the point of leverage. Add to this the iron bar. This is your intelligence, your openness to approach life in a different way. By using intelligence and openness to pivot on the fulcrum of love and trust, you can easily move the previously unmovable - you; an action that supports, sustains, and transforms.

This approach enables heart/intelligence to easily move the heavy weight of your subconscious resistance.

Brain/intellect will endlessly argue and discuss the ways and means of shifting the boulder, but they will never move the weight. Why? Because they created the boulder, and inadvertently, they have generated the energy to maintain it.

SUMMARY

Attaining true prosperity is a process of transformation. Just as the caterpillar is unaware of its magnificent potential, equally, most people live this way. Just as the caterpillar is born to go through a physical metamorphosis, so too, you are born to go through a spiritual transformation. The consciousness of the caterpillar contains its butterfly self, just as your magnificent divinity is held in the daily person whom you are. Are you ready for the transformation? Can you accept that this is your birthright? Can you put in the effort needed to unleash your magnificent self? The caterpillar has an in-built biological trigger for its transformation, but you have to make - and live - this supreme conscious choice.

You are a magnificent human Being. This is Truth! All the negative ideas and beliefs you may have about yourself are simply illusion. The sad reality is that you will live them, and suffer from them, even if they are not real, simply because you have that power. *You do create your own reality.* If your view and perception of your reality is fearful and negative, that is what you will live. But that is not the real you. The real you has the power to change your life.

The real you is truly magnificent. How does that feel? Do you feel it? Does something deep within you stir at the thought and feeling? Does some deep inner longing bubble up, an excitment, a feeling of inner knowing? Can you accept that you are far, far more than you have ever dreamed? Be true to the submerged giant within. Dare to let that Giant Self come to the surface. Dare to allow that giant power - that for so long has frightened you - to destroy your old life, building you a new one. If you live true to your quintessential Self, you are living in the Playing Field of Miracles. And *you* are the miracle!

REMEMBER . . .

Remember . . . true prosperity includes your emotional well-being, your mental balance, and your physical health, as well as a sound financial platform.

Remember . . . everything that you learn about prosperity in your life must be actively realised. If it is not consciously engaged then it is not happening in your life.

Remember . . . to be aware of what you strive for in life. Be aware of the cost on an emotional, physical health, and relationship level.

Remember . . . people who understand that money is no more than a tool of wealth hold the potential to experience true prosperity. People who believe that money itself is true prosperity have a minefield of disappointment ahead of them.

Remember . . . true prosperity and abundance are about you, the person, not the money.

Remember . . . while you see the answers to your financial problems - any problems - as outside of yourself, you will never achieve true prosperity.

Remember . . . your most constant thoughts and spoken words are your focus, and what you focus on is what you attract.

Remember . . . you are part of the 'web of life.' How you treat other people is how you treat yourself. What you express into life is the substance of what you will receive from it.

Remember . . . true prosperity and abundance is something that you program into, or out of, your life. And into or out of is happening all the time!

Remember . . . to repeat with every money transaction, "There is plenty more money where this comes from." Preferably, say it aloud while focussing on a feeling of excitement at knowing that what you are saying is creating your new reality.

Remember . . . as much as is possible - and you decide this - choose employment where you can be happy and fulfilled. Never be fear driven. A fear focus will deny abundance.

Remember . . . many of life's harder, more difficult lessons are designed for soul growth. This too, is part of the true prosperity package.

Remember . . . appreciation is a power. If you wait to receive from life before you begin to appreciate, you will wait a long tme. Develop an attitude of genuine gratitude. It will attract ever more into your life to be grateful for.

Remember . . . happiness comes from the inside-out, not the outside-in. Happiness attracts the fortunate opportunities that lead to abundance.

Remember . . . abundance and true prosperity only exist in the moment. It is important to always think 'from' prosperity and abundance. Never think 'to' it, or 'of' it.

Remember . . . avoid people who think and talk, "I can't afford." It is far more difficult to attract abundance when mixing with and surrounded by people attracting poverty.

Remember . . . appreciaton and trust in life pay regular deposits of prosperity into your abundance account, while all the many expressions of fear only withdraw from it.

Remember . . . old and rigid ways will not serve you. Practice flexibility and trust while learning to embrace new ways. You cannot trust and be anxious.

Remember . . . abundance means a full and benevolent heart. Cultivate ways of expressing the fullness of your heart and you are on the path of true prosperity.

Remember . . . that you own your thoughts, and that you get to experience their energy and contents. For better or worse, this is the way of manifestation. For example, thinking "I can't afford," will manifest financial poverty. Thinking "There is plenty more money where this comes from," will manifest financial abundance.

Remember . . . in every conversation you are either attracting abundance into your life and bank account, or you are emptying it out. Negative words of fear, anxiety and apathy empty it out, while positive words of appreciation, capabability, and self-assurance fill the bank account of life.

Remember . . . your life and your financial income is your creation. If you do not like it the way it is, exercise your right to change it. Change the cause - you - and you can change the expression . This may require effort!

Remember . . . your enthusiam and passion are mighty powers. Cultivate them, and focus them into your life and living, this will transform your life.

Remember . . . none of the above, or anything in this book requires you to be clever. All you need is the will, the focus, and the action.

Remember . . . true prosperity is a state of consciousness. You can create this conscious state by knowing that you can do it. If you think that you can't, you are right!

Remember . . . you are unique, a one-off. Be inspired by other people, learn from other people, but never copy other people. Allow your individuality its true expression.

Remember . . . you are your greatest asset. You, not money! Manage self correctly and wealth is also catered for. When your focus is to only manage wealth, then all too easily relationships and/or self can die from neglect.

Remember . . . you are a wholistic Being. When you live your life in terms of wholeness you are living in harmony with the universe. This is infinitely wiser than living against it!

Remember . . . everything that you have learned in this book must be lived to become a real experience in your life. Neither the book nor the words can do anything for you. You have the ability to achieve anything that you are prepared to focus your energy on.

Remember . . . you are the energy. If you want the results, it's all up to you!

For more information about
Michael J. Roads'
Re*treats, seminars or CD's
please contact:

The Roadsway
3029 Prospect Avenue East
Cleveland, OH 44115
216.588.0099
roadsway@nacs.net

or visit
michaelroads.com

Roadsway Resources

*To provide a foundation for spiritual growth
based on the Self-empowering Principles of Truth*

CD's • Booklets • Newsletter • Books

Talks Available on CD - Recorded Live

<u>Oneness of All Life</u> - Michael discusses oneness vs. separation, accidents vs. purposes, newness, consciousness, and Time-Life and the Human Cycle (birth, death, rebirth, past, future. . .)

<u>The Wholistic Self</u> - Michael discusses the Shadow Self and the Light Self, and how to stay focused in the Light Self.

<u>The Power of Spoken Words</u> - Michael discusses intellect/ intelligence, blame/forgiveness, acceptance, self-criticism, attachments.

<u>Taking Back Your Power #1 and #2</u> (Double CD) - Michael discusses consensus reality, trusting Self and life, living in the moment, and a description of our universe/reality system.

<u>Self Healing #1 and #2 (Double CD)</u> - Michael discusses self-criticism, toxic thoughts, feeling not good enough, food and food vibrations.

<u>Living With Trust</u> - Michael discusses trust vs. anxiety, self-criticism, finding trust within you and trusting yourself.

<u>The Heart Connection</u> - Michael talks about thinking from the heart instead of the brain, the effects of criticism, heart communication and heart "attacks."

<u>Relationships and Sexuality</u> - Michael discusses relationships with partners and Self, his own sexuality, and our relationship with God, including the belief of separation.

<u>God and You</u> - Michael discusses beliefs and concepts about God that we learned as we grew up and a description of his concept of God and Creation. Includes the story of Michael's Awakening.

<u>The Movement of Consciousness in Nature</u> - Michael discusses onlookers vs. participants, onlookers as victims, direct knowing, emotions, and exploration of consciousness in different forms.

<u>Nature Spirits</u> - Michael discusses imagination, fear, growth experiences, letting go of conditioning, and how experiences in the metaphysical are different for everyone.

<u>Metaphysics of Nature #1 and #2 (Double CD)</u>- Michael discusses intellect/intelligence, looking at/seeing, doing to/ being with, consciousness, oneness of all life, newness, the need to move past the intellect to connect with nature, to be in the moment.

<u>Observations of Nature</u> - Michael discusses the physical and metaphysical sides of connecting with nature, awareness and consciousness in your relationship with nature.

<u>The Path #1 and #2 (Double CD)</u> - Treenie tells the story of her path to Enlightenment, beginning with her childhood in England. She also discusses trust, self discipline, thoughts, words, and observing.

<u>Living in Oneness</u>
Michael discusses how everything in life connects, there is nothing outside of Self, how our relationship with self is our relationship with life, and offers positive life-affirming ways to live.

Inner-Exercises Available on CD - Recorded Live

<u>Expansion of Self Light Exercises</u> - A series of four exercises on one CD to practice moving into and expanding your Light Self.

<u>Aspects of Self</u> - An opportunity to dialogue with other aspects of yourself, to hear their perceptions, wisdom and insights.

<u>Dialogue With Self</u> - A dialogue with your own persona of criticism and with appreciation, to learn from them and to find where they can take you.

<u>Expanding Your Sensory Abilities</u> - Exploring your senses to become involved in the complete experience of each sense.

<u>Spirits of Nature</u> - Exploring metaphysical nature through a glade, a forest and animals, finding insights and trust.

<u>The Secret Garden Revisited </u>- Explore and experience your own secret garden, finding your path of Trust to the inner sanctum.

<u>Portrait Gallery</u> - Using your intuition, memory and emotions as you view portraits of yourself at different ages, and members of your family.

<u>Pool of Healing</u> - An opportunity to change painful memories, to resolve the trauma so you feel whole and healed.

<u>Healing Relationships</u> - An opportunity to meet with someone with whom you are currently having difficulties, and with a person who died with things unresolved between you, to heal these relationships.

<u>The Heart House</u> - An opportunity to explore different floors of your Heart House, to see who is there, what they are doing, and what they have to tell you or show you.

Letting Go of Burdens - Following your path of Trust to a place where you can unload all the burdens that have weighed you down, all the worries, anger, fears, everything, so that the Light can consume them.

Tree of Life - Letting go of everything you no longer need and opening to new potential and a greater reality.

Releasing Old Belief Systems - This exercise enables you to release old belief systems that are no longer self-honoring.

Sphere of Tranquility (from *Getting There*) - This exercise takes you to a peaceful, calm place where you can heal whatever you would like to heal.

"Principals of Truth" Booklets

Five individual booklets of condensed wisdom written by Michael. They are packaged together in a boxed set and make great inserts into letters or greeting cards. The booklets are entitled*: "Self Awareness," "True Prosperity," "Wholistic Health," "Self Empowerment"* and *"Meaningful Relationships."*

The Roadsway Newsletter

Subscribe to the quarterly publication that will keep in you in touch with Michael and Treenie. The newsletter contains up-to-date tour information, articles by Michael and Treenie, Inquires and Insights, and more, and is published in January, April, July, and October. Subscriptions can be fulfilled via regular mail or e-mail.

Sample copy sent upon request.

Books

- *Talking With Nature ~ Journey Into Nature, A Michael Roads Reader 1985/1990*
- *Journey Into Oneness, 1994*
- *Into A Timeless Realm , 1995*
- *Getting There*, a novel, *1998*
- *The Magic Formula, 2003*

For a complete order form
and current price list please contact:

The Roadsway
3029 Prospect Avenue East
Cleveland, OH. USA
216.588.0099
866.409.3434 (toll free)
216.391.1636 fax
roadsway@nacs.net
or
www.michaelroads.com